LIMA

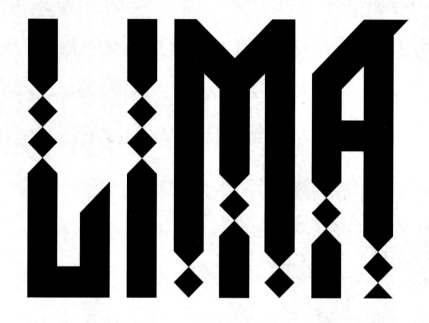

THE COOKBOOK

PERUVIAN
HOME COOKING

VIRGILIO MARTINEZ
& LUCIANA BIANCHI

MITCHELL BEAZLEY

An Hachette UK Company
www.hachette.co.uk

First published in Great Britain in 2015 by Mitchell
Beazley, a division of Octopus Publishing Group Ltd
Carmelite House, 50 Victoria Embankment
London EC4Y 0DZ

www.octopusbooks.co.uk

Luciana Bianchi & Mulato 8 Ltd assert their moral rights
to be identified as the authors of this work.

ISBN 978 1 78472 042 1

A CIP catalogue record for this book is available from
the British Library.

Printed and bound in China

10 9 8 7 6 5 4 3 2 1

Text by Virgilio Martinez & Luciana Bianchi

Publisher: Alison Starling
Managing Editor: Sybella Stephens
Creative Director: Jonathan Christie
Designer: Pene Parker
Photography: Erick Andía Pomar (Lima)
 & The Gaztronome (London)
Props and Food Styling: Luciana Bianchi
Assistant Production Manager: Caroline Alberti

CONTENTS

Lima is a city where all the native Peruvian culture and its immigrant influences meet, and where that cultural diversity is translated into hearty food. It's a fascinating, intriguing place, both modern and ancient, cosmopolitan and provincial, luxurious and humble all at the same time. Bursting with restaurants and vibrant authentic markets, it is the gastronomic heart of Peru and the central reference point for Latin American cuisine today. Here you will find most of the fine dining restaurants in the country, as well as the traditional family restaurants, *cevicherías* and street food. Although it's a busy and chaotic capital city, in some of its corners it can become a gentle, relaxed town. In that way, there are many 'little Limas' co-existing within this large city, which is characterized by its contrasts and paradoxes and its open invitation to all food lovers.

Despite its many imperfections – including the constant grey weather! – Lima is my home and has made me who I am. For me, cooking is a way of sharing my relationship with my country, my city and my personal experiences. I will forever treasure fond memories of the comforting dishes my grandmother would prepare. She cooked simply, always using fresh ingredients, and her dishes featured traditional flavours, to which she added an extra dash of love. My family history is steeped in such precious food moments, which make me happy when eating these dishes as they bring back deep emotions.

So what does Peruvian food mean to my generation? How does the cuisine of my grandparents and their parents influence my culinary thinking today? In recognizing the significance of the emotional ingredient in my grandmother's simple dishes in my own life, which turned them into unforgettable experiences for me, I have come to realize how much this aspect of food is key in transforming a good meal into a memorable event for everyone. What unites us around the table is, above all, our desire to share happy moments. And as our cuisine is an integral part of our culture, many aspects of our identity are reflected in the way we cook.

Modern Peruvian cuisine has two strong roots: first, the Incas, and secondly, the Spanish. After the arrival of the Spanish, a new ethnic group and consequently a new cuisine – the *criollo* (creole) – emerged, which marked the beginning of a whole new chapter in Peruvian culinary history.

We are lucky in Peru to have access to a vast variety of foods throughout the year. In fact, Peru's biodiversity is incomparable to any other place on earth. This is because of our privileged geographical position, with each region of our country offering many different climatic conditions and countless products on a regular basis. The highlands of Peru produce most of the main products of the Peruvian staple diet, including various types of corn, potato, cassava and oca. Parallel to the Pacific Ocean, the Andes has the city of Cuzco as its focus, and its numerous microclimates result in a miraculous natural food larder – a dream come true for anyone who loves to cook! The Amazonian forest, which makes up 60 per cent of the country, provides us with an abundance of unique tropical products. Some of them are available in markets, while others remain a mystery even to most Peruvians. The north coast is renowned for its great seafood, while the southern Pacific coastal area is the ideal region for growing grapes for our national drink – pisco. Here the celebrated regional cuisine of Arequipa can also be found, famous for its *picanterías* – traditional restaurants now officially acknowledged to be part of Peru's cultural heritage.

Over and above this wealth of produce, modern Peruvian cuisine is the result of a cross-cultural culinary exchange between foreign immigrants and native Peruvians, resulting in new flavours and new dishes – an evolutionary process that is still ongoing today. We are children of native groups, and also of Europeans, Asians (mostly Japanese and Chinese), Africans and Arabs. Multiculturalism is integral to our make-up, and so is our cuisine – a fusion of a rich variety of cultural experiences and influences from both a distant and near past. All Peruvians share a passion for delicious food and its association with generosity and comforting memories.

This is not a book about traditional Peruvian cuisine but about traditional Peruvian flavours and heritage revisited from a contemporary perspective. The recipes offer a modern take on emblematic Peruvian produce and classic dishes, and reveal the various facets of my native city in its mix of culinary inheritance and 21st-century urban feeling. My intention here has been to translate Peruvian home cooking into a new modern language while retaining the essential comfort factor that makes us happy at the table. These recipes are accessible to people all over the world, who can try the dishes at home using their local produce.

Virgilio Martinez

LIMA was born out of a friendship and from a desire to bring a new culinary language to London. This city, famous for its multicultural heart, was the perfect place to establish our concept restaurant LIMA, whose aim was to offer the new Peruvian cuisine – young, colourful, exciting, healthy and, above all, delicious.

Our team was perfect for the new venture. We are two brothers from Venezuela now settled in London, Virgilio, the new face of Peruvian cuisine who was born and raised in Lima, and Robert, a Peruvian chef from a small town in the Amazonian area with a strong family tradition in the kitchen.

Our idea was to make LIMA a collaborative project, combining our different strengths to create a unique result, like a new urban music band crafting its own individual sound. And so this experimental restaurant project called LIMA opened its doors in 2012 and has turned out to be a great success, more than we ever expected. But we now understand, after having opened our second restaurant LIMA Floral, the essence of that success – we have developed an authentic and modern cuisine free from cliché.

Today, we regard our restaurants as though they were two different album releases from our band. Both of them have their own sound, as well as an overall style drawing from recognizable core ideas.

London is a global city, open to different foods and ideas, and constantly seeking new authentic experiences. Our new Peruvian cuisine has brought with it the vibes of cosmopolitan Lima, the number one destination for food lovers in Latin America. LIMA restaurants have one mission – to present Peruvian food and culture that reflect the Peruvian table of today. This cookbook celebrates both Lima and London – two vibrant and exceptional cities united by the same passion for great food.

Jose Luis Gonzalez   Virgilio Martinez   Gabriel Gonzalez   Robert Ortiz

DRINKS & SNACKS

Chifle, Camote y Chips de Papa

PLANTAIN, SWEET POTATO AND POTATO CRISPS

A plantain resembles a banana but is bigger, longer, has a thicker skin and is starchier. It is always eaten cooked, baked or fried. Potatoes originate from the Andes, and there are more than 4,000 varieties registered in Peru. They are an excellent low-fat source of carbohydrate. In this recipe you can enjoy all three ingredients together in a delicious snack with dips.

Serves 4

rapeseed oil, for deep-frying
sea salt flakes

PLANTAIN CRISPS
2 large green plantains, peeled

SWEET POTATO CRISPS
3 sweet potatoes, with skins on, washed and dried

BLUE POTATO CRISPS
4 blue potatoes, with skins on, washed and dried

TO SERVE
Avocado Dip (see page 94)
Queso Fresco and Huacatay Herb Cream (see page 94)

1 For the plantain crisps, using a mandolin or sharp knife, slice the plantains lengthways. Soak the plantain strips in iced water for about 20–30 minutes.

2 Heat 500ml rapeseed oil in a deep-fat fryer, or a deep, heavy-based saucepan until it registers 170°C on a sugar thermometer.

3 Drain the plantain strips thoroughly and transfer to kitchen paper to dry.

4 Fry the strips, in small batches, for about 5–6 minutes or until crisp and golden brown. Transfer to a platter lined with kitchen paper and season to taste with sea salt flakes. Keep the cooked batches hot in the oven while cooking the remainder.

5 For both the sweet potato and blue potato crisps, heat 500ml rapeseed oil in a deep-fat fryer, or a deep, heavy-based saucepan until it registers 170°C on a sugar thermometer.

6 Meanwhile, cut the sweet potatoes and potatoes in half lengthways. Using a mandolin or sharp knife, slice thinly.

7 Gently drop a handful of the slices into the oil at a time and fry for 5–6 minutes or until they turn slightly brown. Transfer to a platter lined with kitchen paper and season to taste with sea salt flakes. Keep the cooked batches hot in the oven while cooking the remainder.

8 Serve hot with Avocado Dip and Queso Fresco and Huacatay Herb Cream.

Drinks & Snacks

Yuca Frita

FRIED CASSAVA STICKS

Known as yuca in Peru, cassava is one of the best-loved roots in many Latin American countries. In the Peruvian Amazon area, you will find it mostly in stews and as a simple side dish, prepared in the same way as boiled potatoes. Fried cassava is also very popular in Peru as a snack.

Makes 16 sticks; serves 4

1kg cassava, washed, peeled and cut into 10cm pieces
1 teaspoon fine sea salt
1 litre rapeseed oil, for deep-frying
sea salt flakes (optional)

1 Place the cassava in a saucepan with the fine salt and cover with water. Bring to the boil and cook over a medium heat for about 10 minutes or until the cassava pieces can be easily pierced with a knife.

2 Drain the cassava pieces and transfer to a platter lined with kitchen paper to dry.

3 Heat the oil in a deep-fat fryer, or a deep, heavy-based saucepan until it registers 170°C on a sugar thermometer and fry the cassava, in batches, for 5–6 minutes or until golden brown and crispy.

4 Transfer the fried cassava to a plate lined with kitchen paper to absorb the excess oil. Leave to drain for 4–5 minutes, then season to taste with sea salt flakes, if desired, before serving.

Canchita y Limón

CANCHA CORN AND LIME

Cancha corn kernels are a type of Peruvian popping corn.
The original word is *kamcha* which comes from the Quechua
language, meaning 'toasted corn'. This ancestral Andean snack –
the favourite snack of Peruvians – is served to accompany drinks
before lunch or dinner. Cancha corn is also added to ceviche to
give a crunchy contrast to the dish (see page 104).

Serves 5

2 tablespoons rapeseed oil

150g cancha corn kernels

1 tablespoon sea salt flakes

2–3 limes, cut into quarters,
to serve

1 Heat the rapeseed oil in a large frying pan over a medium-high heat for 1–2 minutes. Add the corn kernels, cover with a lid and reduce the heat to medium. Once you hear the kernels begin to pop, shake the pan to prevent the kernels at the bottom from burning.

2 Cook for about 5 minutes or until the kernels have stopped popping and are deep golden brown. Transfer to a plate lined with kitchen paper to drain.

3 Scatter the corn kernels with the sea salt flakes and serve with the juice from the lime quarters squeezed over.

Camote con Miel de Manzanilla

SWEET POTATO WITH CHAMOMILE HONEY

The sweet potato is in fact not a potato, but a root vegetable and unlike a regular potato all parts of the plant are edible. It is a great source of vitamins A and C, as well as providing 'good' (complex) carbohydrates and dietary fibre. The medicinal properties of chamomile flowers have been recognized for centuries, especially as a relaxation and digestion aid. Combined, they make this dish both a healthy and delicious snack.

Serves 4

1 bunch, about 10g, fresh chamomile flowers or dried chamomile flowers, plus extra fresh petals to garnish
5 tablespoons clear honey
500ml rapeseed oil
2 sweet potatoes

1 Carefully remove the stems from the chamomile flowers.

2 Heat the honey gently in a saucepan. Add the chamomile flowers to the warm honey, stir and cover with a lid. Keep over a low heat for 15 minutes.

3 Peel the sweet potatoes and cut into 2cm cubes.

4 Place the sweet potato cubes in a saucepan and cover with water. Bring to the boil and cook over a medium heat for about 10 minutes or until the sweet potato pieces can be easily pierced with a knife, then drain.

5 Meanwhile, heat the rapeseed oil in a deep-fat fryer or deep, heavy-based saucepan over a medium heat until it registers about 175°C on a sugar thermometer.

6 When the oil has reached the required temperature carefully place the sweet potato cubes in the oil. Cook, turning to brown them evenly on all sides, for about 10 minutes.

7 Remove from the oil and drain in a colander lined with kitchen paper.

8 Strain the honey, then brush the hot fried sweet potato cubes with the infused honey and serve on a platter sprinkled with fresh chamomile petals.

DAVID DEL CURTO S.A.

A visit to a Peruvian market will always be an exciting experience, as the country is famous for its delicious fresh fruit. Luckily, many Peruvian fruits are available outside of Peru, and when ripe they are perfect for whizzing up healthy smoothies and creative alcohol-free cocktails.

Batido de Plátano y Semillas de Cacao

BANANA AND CACAO NIB SMOOTHIE

Serves 3–4

600ml milk
2 ripe bananas, peeled and roughly chopped
25g soft light brown sugar
1 teaspoon cacao nibs, plus extra (optional) to garnish
140g ice cubes

1 Place all the ingredients in a blender and blend on a high speed until smooth.
2 Serve in glasses of your choice, garnished with extra cacao nibs if desired.

Batido de Chirimoya y Naranja Asada

CHERIMOYA AND ROASTED ORANGE SMOOTHIE

Serves 4

4 oranges

250g ripe cherimoya (custard apple)

125ml filtered water

2 teaspoons clear honey

140g ice cubes

1 Preheat the oven to 180°C, Gas Mark 4.

2 Place the whole oranges on a baking sheet and roast for 15 minutes, then leave to cool.

3 Meanwhile, peel the cherimoya and discard the seeds, then chop the flesh into pieces.

4 Cut the cooled oranges in half, reserving one slice per glass for the garnish, and juice the orange halves – you will need about 250ml juice.

5 Strain the orange juice into a blender, add the cherimoya with the other ingredients and blend on a high speed until smooth.

6 Serve in glasses, garnished with the reserved roasted orange slices.

Drinks & Snacks

Batido de Leche de Quinua y Frutos Rojos

QUINOA MILK AND BERRY SMOOTHIE

Serves 3–4

35g white quinoa, cooked and cooled (see page 58)

250g mixed ripe fresh berries, plus extra to garnish

2 tablespoons clear honey

500ml filtered water

250g ice cubes

1 Place all the ingredients in a blender and blend on a high speed until smooth and frothy.

2 Serve garnished with your favourite berries.

Granizado de Limón y Chía

ICED LIME AND CHIA SMOOTHIE

The highly nutritious chia seed is regarded as a superfood – it is particularly rich in omega-3 fatty acids – and is often used in cereal bars and granolas as well as smoothies. A member of the mint family, chia has been cultivated since pre-Columbian times. When soaked its seeds produce a distinctive gel that adds an interesting texture to dishes and drinks.

Serves 4

55g soft light brown sugar
500ml water
25ml freshly squeezed lime juice
140g ice cubes
2 teaspoons chia seeds
1 lime

1 Place the sugar, the water, lime juice and ice cubes in a blender and blend on a high speed until smooth.

2 Add the chia seeds to the smoothie and leave the mixture to rest for 5 minutes to hydrate the chia seeds – they will puff up.

3 Meanwhile, cut the lime into slices.

4 Pour the smoothie into glasses, and using a fork, push the lime slices down the sides of each glass to garnish.

Virgilio's Tip

Mix 1 tablespoon chia seeds with 3 tablespoons water, and you will have a vegan substitute for an egg to use in your recipes.

Batido de Mango y Menta Fresca

MANGO AND FRESH MINT SMOOTHIE

Serves 4

230g ice cubes

250ml unsweetened almond milk

7g mint leaves, a few reserved to garnish

4 tablespoons freshly squeezed lime juice

1 large ripe mango, stoned, peeled and roughly chopped

1 tablespoon soft light brown sugar

1 Place all the ingredients in a blender and blend on a high speed until smooth.

2 Serve the smoothie in glasses garnished with the reserved mint leaves.

Ponche de Quinua de Doña Blanca

QUINOA PUNCH

This is a recipe from my mother – Doña Blanca. It is a healthy and comforting drink made by mixing the superfood quinoa with *choclos* – a white corn with large and creamy grains. This famous oversized Andean corn is pale in colour and less sweet than regular sweetcorn. As well as featuring in this punch, it accompanies many Peruvian dishes, and is also served on the cob as a popular street food in Peru.

Serves 4

40g white quinoa

750ml full-fat milk

220g soft light brown sugar

100g fresh Peruvian white sweetcorn (choclos) kernels or fresh regular sweetcorn kernels

1 Rinse the quinoa in cold running water until the water runs clear, then drain.

2 Place 500ml of the milk, the sugar, corn kernels and quinoa in a saucepan with a tight-fitting lid, cover and bring to the boil over a medium heat. Stir, re-cover and reduce the heat to low. Cook for about 15 minutes – the quinoa is ready when you can see a little ring on the outside of the grain and it is soft.

3 Leave the quinoa mixture to stand off the heat for 5 minutes.

4 Warm the additional 250ml milk in a separate pan and add to the quinoa mixture. Serve the punch hot.

Leche de Quinua

QUINOA MILK

An ancient Andean pseudo-cereal that was revered by the Incas, quinoa is regarded as a superfood because of its health-promoting properties – packed with protein, it contains most of the essential amino acids, is high in dietary fibre and a good source of iron, potassium and magnesium. It's also gluten free.

Makes 710ml

260g white quinoa
750ml filtered water,
plus an extra 500ml

1 Place the quinoa and 750ml filtered water in a saucepan with a tight-fitting lid, cover and bring to the boil over a medium heat. Stir, re-cover and reduce the heat to low. Cook for about 15 minutes – the quinoa is ready when you can see a little ring on the outside of the grain and it is soft.

2 Transfer the cooked quinoa to a blender, add the 500ml filtered water and blend on a high speed until well combined.

3 Pass the mixture twice through a fine-mesh sieve before serving or using in dishes.

Cóctel de Naranja y Aloe Vera

ORANGE AND ALOE COCKTAIL

Serves 4

4 oranges
40g fresh aloe vera leaf (you
need 20g prepared aloe vera gel),
plus extra to garnish (optional)
2 teaspoons clear honey
300g ice cubes
edible flowers, to garnish
(optional)

1 Squeeze the juice from the oranges into a bowl.

2 Using a sharp knife, slice the skin of the aloe vera leaf
and open to reveal the gel. Scoop the aloe vera gel out with
a spoon into a blender.

3 Strain the orange juice into the blender, add the honey
and ice cubes and blend on a high speed for 1 minute.

4 Strain and serve garnished with an aloe leaf and an edible
flower, if liked.

Cóctel de Maracuyá y Hierbaluisa

PASSION FRUIT AND LEMON GRASS COCKTAIL

Serves 4

120ml passion fruit pulp
3 lemon grass stalks,
roughly chopped
340ml filtered water
35ml simple syrup
(see Virgilio's Tip on page 37)
3 ice cubes

1 Place all the ingredients
in a blender and blend
on a high speed until
well combined, then serve.

Cóctel de Cedrón y Achiote

LEMON VERBENA AND ANNATTO SEED COCKTAIL

Achiote, also known as annatto, is a small tree that grows 5–10 metres in height. Prickly red pods grow at the ends of its branches, each containing 30–50 seeds. The seeds are covered with an orange-yellow dye, sometimes used as body make-up by native communities in the Amazon, and also as a food colouring. A small achiote tree can produce up to 270kg of seeds.

Serves 4

1 litre filtered water
20 lemon verbena leaves, plus 4 sprigs to garnish
1 tablespoon annatto (achiote) seeds
1 tablespoon freshly squeezed lime juice
1 tablespoon clear honey
20ml grenadine syrup
ice cubes, to serve

1 Heat the water in a saucepan to boiling point.

2 Add the lemon verbena leaves and annatto (achiote) seeds, then remove from the heat and leave to cool and infuse.

3 Once cooled, add the lime juice and strain.

4 Mix with the honey, grenadine and a couple of ice cubes, pour into glasses and garnish each with a sprig of lemon verbena.

Pisco is the national drink of Peru. It is consumed in its pure form or in cocktails and is also used for cooking. This unique distilled drink is made from grapes and is produced in a similar way to Cognac using copper pot stills but without the ageing process in wooden barrels. There are three types of original Peruvian pisco: puro, mosto verde and acholado (blends). For cocktails, you should use puro or acholado pisco. Mosto verde pisco should be drunk in its pure form, just as you would a fine Cognac.

Pisco Sour

PISCO SOUR

Serves 1

90ml pisco Quebranta
70ml freshly squeezed
lemon juice
35ml Simple Syrup
(see Virgilio's Tip)
1 egg white
8 ice cubes
2 drops of Angostura bitters,
to garnish

1 Add all the ingredients
except the bitters to
a cocktail shaker.
2 Shake for approximately
13 seconds.
3 Strain and serve in a
stemless Martini glass.
4 Garnish with the
Angostura bitters and
serve immediately.

Virgilio's Tip
*Simple syrup can easily be
made at home using equal
quantities of caster sugar and
water. Heat the mixture in a
saucepan until the sugar has
completely dissolved. Set aside
to cool before using it.*

1 Add all the ingredients except the bitters to a cocktail shaker.

3 Strain into a glass.

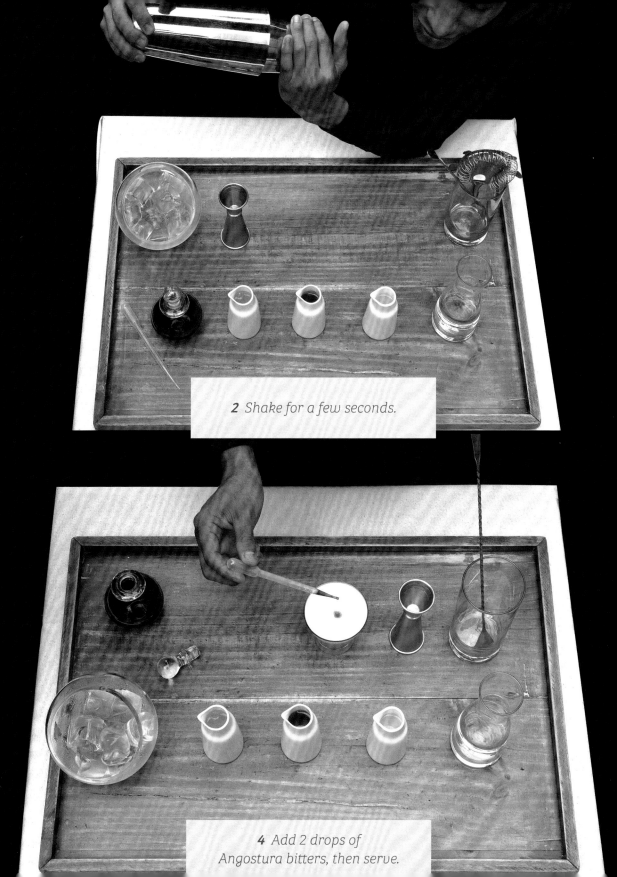

2 *Shake for a few seconds.*

4 *Add 2 drops of Angostura bitters, then serve.*

Señor de Sipán

SEÑOR DE SIPÁN

Serves 1

COCKTAIL
3 ice cubes, for chilling the glass
2 tablespoons apple juice
1 tablespoon raspberry syrup
1 teaspoon pisco Quebranta
Prosecco or Champagne, chilled, for topping up
edible flowers or petals, to garnish

CAMPARI AND PISCO FOAM
500ml double cream or vegan cream
250ml Simple Syrup (see Virgilio's Tip, page 37)
175ml pisco
75ml Campari

1 Add the ice cubes to the Champagne flute for serving and swirl until the glass becomes frosty, then discard the ice.

2 To make the cocktail, add the apple juice, raspberry syrup and pisco to a cocktail shaker. Shake briefly, then strain into the flute and top up with Prosecco or Champagne.

3 Following the manufacturer's instructions, add the foam ingredients to a 1-litre whipping siphon and add the foam to the top.

4 Garnish with edible flower petals and serve immediately.

Drinks & Snacks

Ponche de Pisco

PISCO PUNCH

Serves 1

10 ice cubes
45ml pisco Quebranta
120ml pineapple juice
1 tablespoon freshly squeezed lemon juice
1 tablespoon finely diced fresh pineapple
flesh, to garnish
Maraschino cherry, to garnish

1 Add the ice cubes, pisco, pineapple juice and lemon juice to a large red wine glass.

2 Place a spoon on the outside of the ice cubes and swirl.

3 Garnish the cocktail with the finely diced fresh pineapple and a Maraschino cherry and serve immediately.

Chilcano de Manzanilla

CHAMOMILE CHILCANO

Serves 1

**CHAMOMILE-INFUSED
PISCO ITALIA**

8g fresh chamomile, plus extra
to garnish

700ml pisco Italia

CHILCANO

5 ice cubes

2 tablespoons freshly squeezed
lemon juice

60ml Chamomile-infused Pisco
Italia (see above)

180ml ginger ale

5 drops of Angostura bitters

2 lemon slices

1 Add the fresh chamomile to a clean 750ml glass bottle, then fill the rest of the bottle with the pisco. Seal and leave to infuse for 2 weeks.

2 Strain and reserve the infused pisco in the bottle.

3 Add the ice cubes to a highball glass, then the lemon juice and the infused pisco.

4 Then add the ginger ale, Angostura bitters and the lemon slices, stir and serve immediately garnished with extra camomile flowers if liked.

Chilcano de Kión

GINGER CHILCANO

Serves 1

2.5cm piece of fresh root ginger
5 ice cubes
60ml pisco Italia
2 tablespoons freshly squeezed lemon juice
180ml ginger ale
5 drops of Angostura bitters
1 thin lemon slice

1 Peel the piece of ginger, then cut it in half. Cut one half into 4 thin slices and reserve.

2 Use a Microplane or fine grater to grate the other ginger half.

3 Add the ice cubes to a highball glass, then add the pisco and lemon juice.

4 Then add the ginger ale, Angostura bitters, the lemon slice and reserved ginger slices.

5 Stir the ingredients together and serve.

Cuento del Diablo

CUENTO DEL DIABLO

Serves 1

25ml pisco Quebranta infused
with chillies (see Virgilio's Tip)
35ml Triple Sec
20ml ready-made strawberry
purée
20ml freshly squeezed
lime juice
10ml grenadine syrup
3–4 ice cubes, for chilling
the glass
2 small red chillies, to garnish

Virgilio's Tip
*Infuse the pisco with 5 fresh, red
Ají Limo chillies (see page 83),
seeds and veins removed, in the
same way as for Chamomile-
infused pisco Italia (see page 42)
for 2–3 weeks. How long you
leave it to infuse depends on
how spicy you wish the pisco
to be.*

1 Add all the ingredients except the ice cubes to a shaker
glass or Boston cocktail shaker, shake and then stir.

2 Add the ice cubes to a Martini glass and swirl until the
glass becomes frosted, then discard the ice. Pour the mixture
into a Martini glass.

3 Make a short lengthways cut in the stalk end of each chilli
to one side of the stalk and place on the rim to look like devil's
horns. Serve immediately.

Mochika

MOCHIKA

Mochica is the name of an ancient civilization of warriors on the coast of Northern Peru. They were skilled architects, and built pyramids, temples, and water systems. They were also famous for making remarkable ceramics.

Serves 1

50ml Ron Cartavio Gold Rum
25ml pineapple juice, chilled
20ml vanilla syrup
20ml passion fruit purée, chilled
3 drops of Angostura bitters
3 mint leaves, plus extra
to garnish
3–4 ice cubes, for chilling
the glass
passion fruit slice, to garnish
(optional)

1 Add all the ingredients to a cocktail shaker, except the ice cubes, and shake vigorously until a thin layer of foam is created. Double strain to remove the mint pieces.

2 Add the ice cubes to a Martini glass and swirl until the glass becomes frosted, then discard the ice.

3 Add the shaken mixture to the glass, garnish with the passion fruit slice, if desired, and mint leaves and serve immediately.

SALADS
& SIDE DISHES

Salteado de Raices y Maíz

SAUTÉED ROOTS AND CORN

Oca is a tuberous stem grown in Peru, rich in iron and vitamin C. It is widely used in South America for baking or cooking, as an alternative to potato. Oca can be cooked, or eaten raw, thinly sliced and served like radish. The greens are edible too, and has a similar taste to sorrel.

Serves 4

150g fresh Peruvian white sweetcorn (choclos) kernels (see page 28) or fresh regular sweetcorn kernels

2 blue potatoes, skin on, washed and cut into quarters

1 large sweet potato, skin on, washed and cut into quarters

2 large ocas or parsnips, skin on, washed and cut in half

8 baby corn cobs

1 tablespoon olive oil

sea salt flakes

150g cooked cancha corn kernels (see page 18), to serve (optional)

1 Place the corn kernels in a saucepan and cover with water. Cover the pan, bring to the boil and cook for about 20 minutes until the kernels can be easily pierced with the tip of a knife. Drain and set aside.

2 Meanwhile, in a separate saucepan, cook the blue potatoes, sweet potato and ocas or parsnips for 10–15 minutes or until they are tender but still firm. Drain and set aside.

3 In another pan, cook the baby corn in boiling water for about 3 minutes or until tender. Drain and leave to cool on kitchen paper.

4 Heat the olive oil in a sauté pan and sauté all the cooked vegetables for about 3 minutes or until they have developed a caramelized crust. Sprinkle with sea salt flakes.

5 Transfer to a serving plate and scatter over the cancha corn, if using.

Chonta Asada y Kiwicha

GRILLED HEARTS OF PALM WITH AMARANTH

Delicate in flavour and texture, fresh hearts of palm are loved in many Latin American countries, and are a highly versatile ingredient. In recent times, Peru has increasingly invested in the sustainable production of hearts of palm to avoid deforestation. Good-quality hearts of palm are readily available in jars and cans, which are suitable for using in this dish. Amaranth is a perennial plant, and is not a cereal despite its looks. It is a gluten-free pseudo-grain similar to quinoa, and is packed with essential amino-acids. It is considered to be one of the world's healthiest foods.

Serves 4

250ml olive oil

150g annatto (achiote) seeds
(see page 33)

100g amaranth (kiwicha) grain

4 hearts of palm from a jar
or can, drained and cut into
3cm pieces

fine sea salt

1 Heat the olive oil in a saucepan until it registers 75°C on a sugar thermometer. Add the annatto (achiote) seeds and then remove the pan from the heat and leave the oil to cool.

2 Transfer the seeds and oil to a blender and blend for 2 minutes, then strain through a fine-mesh sieve.

3 Meanwhile, rinse the amaranth in cold running water until the water runs clear, then drain. Place in a saucepan with a tight-fitting lid, cover with water and bring to the boil over a medium heat. Stir, re-cover and reduce the heat to low. Cook for about 10 minutes until soft.

4 Cook the hearts of palm pieces under a medium-high grill, turning at intervals, until browned, then set aside.

5 Add 4 tablespoons of the annatto oil to the cooked amaranth and season to taste with salt.

6 Spread the amaranth mixture evenly over the grilled hearts of palm and serve warm.

Choclo, Chimichurri y Queso Fresco

CORN, CHIMICHURRI AND QUESO FRESCO

Peruvian queso fresco, a soft, fresh curd cheese with a mild acidity, is produced from cow's milk. It has a texture similar to that of fresh tofu. Chimichurri is a type of salsa or pesto that is popular throughout Latin America, and you will find various versions and local recipes. It is very versatile and can be served both hot and cold.

Serves 4

410g fresh white sweetcorn (choclos) kernels (see page 28) or fresh regular sweetcorn kernels

200g Peruvian queso fresco or fresh mozzarella cheese, cut into small cubes

½ red onion, finely sliced (julienned)

extra herbs and herb flowers (optional), to garnish

CHIMICHURRI

2 tablespoons chopped coriander leaves

2 tablespoons chopped flat leaf parsley leaves

1 teaspoon chopped mint

1 teaspoon fine sea salt

125ml olive oil

1 Place the corn kernels in a saucepan and cover with water. Cover the pan, bring to the boil and cook for about 20 minutes until the kernels can be easily pierced with the tip of a knife. Drain and leave to cool, then cover and refrigerate.

2 To make the chimichurri, place the herbs, salt and olive oil in a blender and blend for 2 minutes.

3 Put the cooked chilled corn, cheese and onion into a serving bowl or arrange it stylishly on a long plate. Add drops of chimichurri, and garnish with extra herbs and herb flowers, if desired.

Quinua Multicolor y Menta

MULTICOLOURED QUINOA AND MINT

Although there are actually 3,000 varieties of quinoa grouped into five categories, the white, red and black are the three most readily available around the world. Sacha inchi oil has a delicate nutty flavour, but argan, groundnut or olive oil can be substituted if you have difficulty sourcing it.

Serves 4

60g red quinoa

60g white quinoa

60g black quinoa

½ small shallot, roughly chopped

juice of ½ lemon

juice of ½ orange

2 tablespoons cider vinegar

1 tablespoon caster sugar

90ml sacha inchi oil, argan oil, groundnut oil or olive oil

½–¾ teaspoon fine sea salt

½ teaspoon freshly ground black pepper

TO GARNISH

4 radishes, thinly sliced

2 black radishes (if available), thinly sliced

mint leaves

1 Rinse the 3 types of quinoa separately in cold running water until the water runs clear, then drain.

2 Place each type of quinoa into separate saucepans with tight-fitting lids and add water to cover by 5cm. Cover with the lid and bring to the boil over a medium heat. Stir, re-cover and reduce the heat to low. Cook for about 15 minutes – the quinoa is ready when you can see a little ring on the outside of the grain and it is soft. Rinse in cold water, then drain and leave to cool.

3 Place all the remaining ingredients into a blender and blend until smooth. Adjust the seasoning if necessary.

4 Once the quinoas have cooled, mix them with the citrus dressing.

5 Place the dressed quinoa on a plate and garnish with the slices of radish and the mint leaves.

Tomates, Aguaymanto y Rúcula con Vinagreta Verde y Amarilla

TOMATOES, PHYSALIS AND ROCKET WITH GREEN AND YELLOW VINAIGRETTE

Serves 4

2 heirloom tomatoes

200g cherry tomatoes

200g rocket leaves

20g physalis (Cape gooseberry), husks removed (prepared weight)

1 Ají Limo chilli (see page 83), jalapeño pepper or other mild chilli

sea salt flakes

GREEN VINAIGRETTE

8 spring onions

2 small garlic cloves, peeled but left whole

60ml rice vinegar

1–2 teaspoons agave nectar or clear honey

120ml olive oil

fine sea salt and freshly ground black pepper

YELLOW VINAIGRETTE

1 large yellow pepper, cored, deseeded and roughly chopped

4 teaspoons red wine vinegar

2 tablespoons extra virgin olive oil

pinch of sugar (optional)

fine sea salt and freshly ground black pepper

Physalis looks somewhat like a yellow cherry tomato encased in a lantern-shaped papery husk and grows at altitudes above 800 metres. It is indigenous to South America but is cultivated throughout the world. Because its flavour is between sweet and slightly tart, it can be used for both savoury and sweet dishes, and is also ideal as a delicious healthy snack.

1 For the green vinaigrette, blanch the spring onions in a saucepan of salted boiling water for 30 seconds. To stop the cooking process, transfer the spring onions to a bowl of iced water for a few minutes, then remove.

2 Place the spring onions with the garlic and rice vinegar in a blender and blend until smooth. Add the agave nectar or honey and salt and pepper to taste. Then, with the blender on a low speed, add the olive oil in a steady stream. Taste and adjust the seasonings as desired. Set aside and clean the blender.

3 For the yellow vinaigrette, place the yellow pepper, red wine vinegar and extra virgin olive oil in the blender and blend until smooth. Season to taste with salt and pepper, and add the sugar if necessary.

4 Cut the tomatoes into different sizes and mix them with the rocket leaves and physalis.

5 Remove the seeds from the chilli and slice into rings.

6 Dress the salad with the 2 vinaigrettes separately, trying not to mix them. Garnish with the chilli slices and sprinkle with salt flakes to taste. The vinaigrettes will keep in the refrigerator, tightly covered, for up to about 3 days.

Bonito, Habas y Pimiento Rojo Asado

BONITO, BROAD BEANS AND ROASTED RED PEPPER

Arequipa, Peru's second most industrialized and commercial city, is famous for its cuisine, and its *picantería* restaurants have been declared a Peruvian cultural heritage. *Solterito* or 'little bachelor' is a salad from these traditional eateries – a comfort dish for many Peruvians that comes in a multitude of versions, this one made with bonito, an oily fish closely related to the tuna.

Serves 4

2 red peppers

½ small garlic clove, chopped

1 tablespoon balsamic vinegar

2 tablespoons extra virgin olive oil

½ teaspoon clear honey

120g broad beans, cooked and cooled

100g queso fresco (see page 56) or fresh mozzarella cheese, cut into small cubes

50g cherry tomatoes, cut into quarters

¼ red onion, finely diced

300g bonito or tuna loin

fine sea salt and freshly ground black pepper

herbs, to garnish (optional)

1 Roast the red peppers directly over a gas flame on the hob or in a very hot oven, turning frequently, until the skins are partially black. Leave to cool in a bowl, covered with a clean tea towel. The peppers should start to sweat after about 15 minutes. Then remove the skin and seeds of the peppers.

2 Place the roasted pepper flesh in a food processor or blender and blend to a purée. Season to taste with salt and pepper.

3 Add the garlic and balsamic vinegar to the food processor or blender. Then, with the processor or blender on a low speed, add 1½ tablespoons of the extra virgin olive oil in a steady stream followed by the honey. Once the mixture is smooth, adjust the seasonings. Set the vinaigrette aside.

4 Gently mix together the broad beans, cheese, cherry tomatoes and red onion, then set aside.

5 Season the bonito or tuna loin with salt. Heat a sauté pan over a high heat, and when hot, add the remaining ½ tablespoon olive oil and sear the fish for 35 seconds each side. Remove from the pan and leave to cool, then cut into thin slices.

6 Place the broad bean salad on a serving plate and top with the fish slices, then drizzle the vinaigrette sparingly over the dish. Garnish with herbs if desired, and serve.

Lechuga Romana con Ají Amarillo y Aliño de Maní en Vez de Aliño, Vinagreta

ROMAINE LETTUCE AND AJÍ AMARILLO WITH PEANUT DRESSING

There are various types of black salt. The most famous of them is Himalayan black salt, also known as Kala Namak – a rock salt from mines often used in Indian cuisine. I've used black lava salt in this recipe (see my Tip below) but if you can't find it just use regular salt instead.

Serves 4

1 head of iceberg lettuce

PEANUT DRESSING

3 tablespoons water

2 tablespoons rice vinegar

1 tablespoon chopped spring onions

1 tablespoon peanut butter

1 tablespoon soy sauce

1 teaspoon peeled and grated fresh root ginger

1 teaspoon dark sesame oil

2 teaspoons roasted peanuts

TO SERVE

1 Ají Amarillo chilli (see page 82) or other mild-medium hot orange or red chilli, very finely sliced

black lava salt or fine sea salt

1 Cut the head of lettuce in half, then trim the base of the halves to create a flat side.

2 To prepare the dressing, place the 3 tablespoons of water, rice vinegar, spring onions, peanut butter, soy sauce, ginger and sesame oil in a blender and blend for about 10 seconds.

3 Add the peanuts and blend until smooth.

4 Dress the lettuce with the peanut dressing, then scatter over the chilli and black lava salt or sea salt to taste.

Virgilio's Tip
Black lava salt is salt that has been blended with activated charcoal and can be sourced from specialist delis and some health food shops.

Salads & Side Dishes

Arroz Andino

ANDEAN RICE

This rice goes particularly well with Chicken and Potato Pachamanca (see page 171) and Sea Bass Sudado (see page 162).

Serves 4

1 tablespoon flat leaf parsley leaves

1 tablespoon coriander leaves

2 garlic cloves, peeled but left whole

1½ teaspoons fine sea salt

3 tablespoons extra virgin olive oil

6 tablespoons water, plus 500ml boiling water

250g medium-grain white rice, such as Bomba paella rice

1 Place the herbs, garlic, salt, 1 tablespoon olive oil and the 6 tablespoons water in a blender or food processor and process until thoroughly puréed.

2 Heat the remaining olive oil in a saucepan over a medium heat, add the rice and cook, stirring, for about 1 minute until the rice turns pale white.

3 Pour in the boiling water and the puréed herb mixture, and stir to combine with the rice.

4 Cover the pan and simmer over a low heat for 20 minutes or until there are air holes visible in the cooked rice.

5 Fluff the rice up with a fork and serve.

Arroz con Choclo Blanco

RICE WITH WHITE CORN

Serves 4

130g fresh Peruvian white
sweetcorn (choclos) kernels
(see page 28) or fresh regular
sweetcorn kernels
1 tablespoon rapeseed oil
370g medium-grain white rice,
such as Bomba paella rice
1 litre boiling water
fine sea salt

1 Rinse and drain the corn
kernels.

2 Heat the rapeseed oil in
a large saucepan over a
medium heat, add the rice
to the oil and cook, stirring,
for about 1 minute until the
rice turns pale white, then
add the corn.

3 Pour in the boiling water
and salt to taste and stir
to combine.

4 Cover the pan and
simmer over a low heat for
20 minutes or until there
are air holes visible in the
cooked rice.

5 Fluff the rice up with
a fork and serve.

Puré de Papa Asada

MASHED BAKED POTATOES

Serve this smooth mash with any slow-cooked stew such as Pork with Chicha de Jora (see page 179).

Serves 4

1kg King Edward or other floury potatoes, with skins on, washed and dried

115g unsalted butter

1 teaspoon sea salt flakes

1 Preheat the oven to 220°C, Gas Mark 7.

2 Wrap each potato in foil. Prick the potatoes through the foil several times with a fork. Bake in the oven for 1–1¼ hours or until tender.

3 Heat the butter with the salt flakes in a heavy-based saucepan over a medium heat or until the butter has melted.

4 Let the baked potatoes cool a little, then unwrap, remove the skins and cut the flesh into quarters. Break the potato quarters with a fork until they are completely mashed, then mix with the melted butter and salt.

Puré Cremoso de Camote

CREAMED SWEET POTATOES

This creamy mash is great served with Short Ribs Anticuchos (see page 166).

Serves 4

6 sweet potatoes, peeled
60g butter, softened
125ml single cream, at room
temperature
¼ teaspoon ground cinnamon
fine sea salt

1 Fill a large saucepan
about three-quarters full of
water, add 1 teaspoon salt
and bring to the boil.

2 Meanwhile, cut the sweet
potatoes in half lengthways,
then cut each half into
quarters to give 8 pieces.
This will help them to cook
more quickly.

3 Add the sweet potatoes
to the boiling water, reduce
the heat and simmer for
15 minutes or until they can
be easily pierced with a knife.

4 Drain the sweet potatoes
and return them to the
pan. Add the butter, cream
and cinnamon, then mash
gently with a potato masher,
season to taste with salt and
mix well.

Papas Moradas con Chimichurri y Papas Nuevas Salteadas con Sal de Maras

CHIMICHURRI WITH BLUE POTATOES AND SAUTÉED NEW POTATOES WITH MARAS SALT

The town of Maras, located in the Sacred Valley of the Incas, is renowned for its salt – Sal de Maras – which has a strong flavour and has been used since pre-Inca times. Underground mineral water surfaces at Maras from the Qoripujio spring where it is collected into 3,000 pools and is harvested by local workers after a natural process of evaporation.

Serves 4

300g small new potatoes, skins on, washed

300g blue potatoes, skins on, washed and cut into quarters

70ml olive oil

fine sea salt

Maras salt or sea salt flakes

CHIMICHURRI

25g chives

30g flat leaf parsley

30g fresh coriander

50ml olive oil

5g (about 2) garlic cloves, peeled but left whole

½ teaspoon salt

½ teaspoon freshly ground black pepper

1 Place all the chimichurri ingredients in a blender and blend to a smooth paste, then set aside.

2 Put the new potatoes and blue potatoes into 2 separate saucepans, cover with cold water and add 1 teaspoon fine sea salt to each. Bring to the boil and cook for about 20 minutes or until tender, then drain, keeping them separate.

3 Heat half the olive oil in a sauté pan, add the blue potatoes and cook gently until evenly browned. Remove to a bowl.

4 Repeat the process with the new potatoes and place them in a separate bowl.

5 Season the blue potatoes with half the chimichurri just before serving. The remaining chimichurri can be stored in the refrigerator or frozen.

6 Season the new potatoes with Maras salt or sea salt flakes to taste and serve.

TIGER'S MILK,
CHILLI PASTES & SAUCES

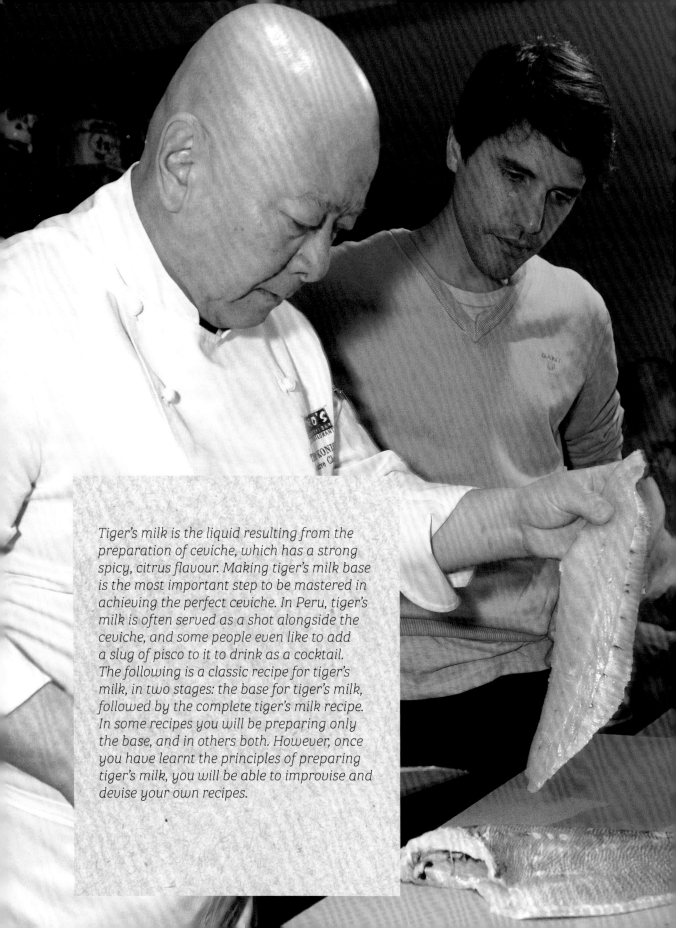

Tiger's milk is the liquid resulting from the preparation of ceviche, which has a strong spicy, citrus flavour. Making tiger's milk base is the most important step to be mastered in achieving the perfect ceviche. In Peru, tiger's milk is often served as a shot alongside the ceviche, and some people even like to add a slug of pisco to it to drink as a cocktail. The following is a classic recipe for tiger's milk, in two stages: the base for tiger's milk, followed by the complete tiger's milk recipe. In some recipes you will be preparing only the base, and in others both. However, once you have learnt the principles of preparing tiger's milk, you will be able to improvise and devise your own recipes.

Leche de Tigre – Base

TIGER'S MILK BASE

Makes 220g

100g celery, roughly chopped

100g onion, roughly chopped

2 garlic cloves, peeled
but left whole

3cm piece of fresh root ginger,
peeled

2 tablespoons fine sea salt

1 teaspoon sugar

100g coriander stems

1 Place all the ingredients except the coriander stems in a blender and blend until puréed.

2 Add the coriander stems to the purée, then leave to marinate in the refrigerator for 1 hour before removing and discarding the coriander.

3 Cover tightly and refrigerate until ready to use in the preparation of Tiger's Milk (see below).

Leche de Tigre – Receta Entera

TIGER'S MILK COMPLETE RECIPE

Makes 400g

juice of 1kg limes (you need about 150ml lime juice)

4 tablespoons Tiger's Milk Base (see above)

30g very fresh skinless white fish fillet

200g ice cubes

1 teaspoon deseeded and finely chopped Ají Limo chilli (see page 83) or pickled jalapeño pepper

fine sea salt

1 Add the lime juice, Tiger's Milk Base, fish and ice cubes to a blender and blend for 1 minute.

2 Strain through a fine-mesh sieve into a non-reactive bowl. Adjust the seasoning with salt and add the chilli.

3 Cover and refrigerate for 5 minutes before using.

Virgilio's Tips

The limes should be freshly juiced whenever you prepare Tiger's Milk, never in advance. Also, never squeeze the limes with a machine but by hand. The complete recipe for Tiger's Milk should always be made fresh and used immediately.

Conchas y Carambolas con Leche de Tigre y Brotes de Quinua

SCALLOPS AND STAR FRUIT WITH TIGER'S MILK AND QUINOA SPROUTS

Serves 4

3 star fruit (carambola), washed

4 tablespoons Tiger's Milk Base (see page 75)

juice of 1kg limes (you need about 150ml lime juice)

200g ice cubes

30g very fresh skinless white fish fillet

1 teaspoon deseeded and finely chopped Ají Limo chilli (see page 83) or pickled jalapeño pepper

8 fresh scallops, shelled and cleaned

fine sea salt

quinoa sprouts, to garnish (optional)

1 Trim off the edges of the ridges and any brown parts of the star fruit. Slice the fruit, discard the seeds and then roughly chop the flesh. Place in a blender and blend to a purée. Strain and pour back into the blender.

2 Add the Tiger's Milk Base, lime juice, ice cubes, fish and chilli and blend for 1 minute.

3 Strain the mixture through a fine-mesh sieve into a non-reactive bowl. Adjust the seasoning with salt.

4 Cover and refrigerate for 5 minutes.

5 Cut the scallops into quarters and pour the tiger's milk mixture over them just before serving. Garnish the dish with quinoa sprouts, if desired.

Almejas con Leche de Tigre de Rocoto

CLAMS WITH ROCOTO TIGER'S MILK

Serves 4

4 tablespoons Tiger's Milk Base
(see page 75)
juice of 1kg limes (you need
about 150ml lime juice)
5 tablespoons Ají Rocoto Paste
(see page 87)
200g ice cubes
30g very fresh skinless white
fish fillet
1 teaspoon deseeded and finely
chopped Ají Limo chilli (see
page 83) or pickled jalapeño
pepper
12 shelled live clams
fine sea salt
amaranth sprouts, to garnish
(optional)

1 Place the Tiger's Milk Base, lime juice, Ají Rocoto Paste, ice cubes, fish and chilli in a blender and blend for 1 minute.

2 Strain through a fine-mesh sieve into a non-reactive bowl. Adjust the seasoning with salt.

3 Cover and refrigerate for 5 minutes.

4 Slice the clams and pour the Tiger's Milk mixture over them just before serving. Garnish the dish with amaranth sprouts, if desired.

Tiger's Milk, Chilli Pastes & Sauces

Leche de Tigre de Aloe Vera

ALOE VERA TIGER'S MILK

Serves 4

120g fresh aloe vera leaf,
plus extra to garnish

4 tablespoons Tiger's Milk Base
(see page 75)

juice of 1kg limes (you need
about 150ml lime juice)

200g ice cubes

1 teaspoon deseeded and finely
chopped Ají Limo chilli (see
page 83) or pickled jalapeño
pepper

fine sea salt

1 Using a sharp knife, cut off the tip of the aloe vera leaf and the spiny edge either side of the leaf. Cut the leaf lengthways in half, separating the back and front. Slice the aloe vera gel away from the skin and cut into small cubes.

2 Place the aloe vera cubes in a blender and blend until liquidized.

3 Add the Tiger's Milk Base, lime juice and ice cubes to the blender and blend for 1 minute.

4 Strain through a fine-mesh sieve into a non-reactive bowl. Adjust the seasoning with salt and add the chilli.

5 Cover and refrigerate for 5 minutes.

6 Serve garnished with a piece of aloe vera leaf.

Leche de Tigre de Mastuerzo

NASTURTIUM TIGER'S MILK

Serves 4

100g nasturtium leaves, washed and dried, plus petals and extra leaves to garnish

120ml cold water

4 tablespoons Tiger's Milk Base (see page 75)

juice of 1kg limes (you need about 150ml lime juice)

200g ice cubes

30g very fresh skinless white fish fillet

fine sea salt

1 Place the nasturtium leaves and the water in a blender and blend until liquidized. Strain through a fine-mesh sieve and clean the blender.

2 Return the nasturtium liquid to the blender, add the Tiger's Milk Base, lime juice, ice cubes and fish and blend for 1 minute.

3 Strain through a fine-mesh sieve. Adjust the seasoning with salt to taste.

4 Serve garnished with the nasturtium petals and leaves.

Leche de Tigre de Espárrago Verde con Maíz Chulpi

ASPARAGUS TIGER'S MILK WITH CHULPI CORN

Serves 4

10 asparagus spears, washed and tough ends trimmed

1 teaspoon olive oil

240ml cold water

4 tablespoons Tiger's Milk Base (see page 75)

juice of 1kg limes (you need about 150ml lime juice)

200g ice cubes

30g very fresh skinless white fish fillet

1 teaspoon deseeded and finely chopped Ají Limo chilli (see page 83) or pickled jalapeño pepper

fine sea salt

1kg cooked cancha corn kernels (see page 18), to serve

1 Place a steamer basket in a saucepan. Fill the pan with water up to the base of the basket and bring to the boil. Add 4 asparagus spears and the olive oil to the steamer basket. Cover and reduce the heat. Steam for 3–5 minutes or until the asparagus is crisp tender and bright green. Set aside to cool.

2 Meanwhile, place the remaining 6 asparagus spears in a blender with the 240ml water and blend until well combined. Strain to remove the remaining fibrous bits of asparagus and reserve the liquid. Clean the blender.

3 Return the asparagus liquid to the blender and add the Tiger's Milk Base, lime juice, ice cubes, fish and chilli and blend for 1 minute.

4 Strain through a fine-mesh sieve into a non-reactive bowl. Adjust the seasoning with salt.

5 Cover and refrigerate for 5 minutes.

6 Slice the steamed asparagus or make shavings using a vegetable peeler and pour the Tiger's Milk over just before serving. Serve with the cancha corn.

Leche de Tigre de Tomate y Pisco

TOMATO JUICE AND PISCO TIGER'S MILK

Serves 4

4 tablespoons Tiger's Milk Base
(see page 75)

juice of 1kg limes (you need
about 150ml lime juice)

200ml tomato juice

40ml pisco

200g ice cubes

30g very fresh skinless white
fish fillet

1 teaspoon deseeded and finely
chopped Ají Limo chilli (see
page 83) or pickled jalapeño
pepper

fine sea salt

1 celery stick, cut into thin
strips, to garnish

1 Place the Tiger's Milk Base, lime juice, tomato juice, pisco, ice cubes, fish and chilli in a blender and blend for 1 minute.

2 Strain through a fine-mesh sieve into a non-reactive bowl. Adjust the seasoning with salt.

3 Cover and refrigerate for 5 minutes.

4 Serve garnished with the celery strips.

Most popular Peruvian Ají chillies

Ají Rocoto

Looking like a miniature pepper, you can buy this chilli in Peru in its unripened green form or ripe, red or yellow in colour. Hot.

Ají Amarillo

The most important chilli of Peru. Despite its name translating as 'yellow chilli', it is usually orange in colour. Mild to medium hot.

Tiger's Milk, Chilli Pastes & Sauces

Ají Limo

There are many varieties in Peru of this highly aromatic chilli, including different shapes and colours ranging from white-yellow, yellow and orange to red, purple and green. Medium-hot to hot.

Ají Panca

More often used dried than fresh, you can buy these in Peru either whole in their dried form or ground as chilli powder. The colour ranges from red to brown. Hot.

Pasta de Ají Amarillo

YELLOW AJÍ PASTE

Makes 400g

500g Ají Limo chillies or any mild-medium yellow chillies (see page 83 and Virgilio's Tip on page 86)

1 teaspoon sugar

1 Cut the chillies in half lengthways and remove the veins and seeds.

2 Wash the chilli halves in 4 changes of fresh water.

3 Place the chillies in a large saucepan, cover with water and add the sugar. Bring to the boil, then reduce the heat and simmer for 8 minutes.

4 Drain and then repeat the simmering process 5 times (but without sugar), changing the water each time.

5 Drain the chillies, place in a blender and blend to a smooth paste. Cover tightly and refrigerate until required, or store in the freezer.

Pasta de Ají Panca

AJÍ PANCA PASTE

Makes 250g

250g dried Ají Panca chillies (see page 83) or Mexican Guajillo chillies

60ml white wine vinegar

375g caster sugar

1 Cut the chillies in half lengthways and remove the veins and seeds.

2 Wash the chilli halves in 4 changes of fresh water with a tablespoon of vinegar added each time.

3 Leave to soak in cold water for 5 hours.

4 Drain the chillies and place in a saucepan, cover with water and add all the sugar. Bring to the boil, then reduce the heat and simmer for 8 minutes.

5 Drain and then repeat the simmering process 5 times (but without sugar), changing the water each time.

6 Drain the chillies, place in a blender and blend to a smooth paste. Cover tightly and refrigerate until required, or store in the freezer.

YELLOW AJÍ PASTE

AJÍ PANCA PASTE

AJÍ ROCOTO PASTE

ONION AND GARLIC PASTE

Virgilio's Tip

The repetition of the simmering process helps to reduce the heat. How many times you need to do this depends on how hot the chillies are, but this is the average number to achieve the appropriate level of heat in the final paste.

If you can't find any Peruvian Ají Amarillo chillies, you can use 450g yellow peppers and 50g red bird's eye (Thai) chillies, but in that case you will only need to repeat the boiling process twice more rather than a further 5 times.

Pasta de Rocoto

AJÍ ROCOTO PASTE

Makes 300g

1kg Ají Rocoto chillies
(see page 82 and Virgilio's Tip,
below)

2 litres water

2 tablespoons sugar

Virgilio's Tip

*Look out for frozen Ají Rocoto
chillies, which may be easier to
source. But if you can't find this
Peruvian variety of chilli, you
can use 700g yellow peppers
and 300g red bird's eye (Thai)
chillies, but you will only need
to repeat the boiling process
3 more times rather than a
further 5 times.*

1 Cut the chillies in half lengthways and remove the veins
and seeds.

2 Wash the chilli halves in 4 changes of fresh water.

3 Place the chillies in a large saucepan, add the water
and sugar and bring to the boil, then reduce the heat
and simmer for 8 minutes.

4 Drain and then repeat the simmering process 5 times (but
without sugar), changing the water each time.

5 Drain the chillies, place in a blender and blend to a smooth
paste. Cover tightly and refrigerate until required, or store
in the freezer.

Aderezo de Ajo y Cebolla

ONION AND GARLIC PASTE

Makes 300g

90ml sunflower oil

250g garlic cloves, peeled
but left whole

1kg onions, cut into large dice

1 Heat the oil in a large sauté pan over a medium heat.
Add the whole garlic cloves and sauté until slightly browned.

2 Add the onions and cook over a low heat for about
40 minutes or until light brown and caramelized.

3 Transfer to a blender and blend to a purée, then pass
through a fine-mesh sieve. Leave to cool, then cover tightly
and refrigerate until required, or store in the freezer.

Chimichurri de Hierbas Andinas

ANDEAN HERB CHIMICHURRI

Makes 320g

30g mint leaves

30g huacatay leaves or 10g
each coriander, tarragon
and basil

25g chincho leaves or 100g flat
leaf parsley

50ml olive oil

1 garlic clove, peeled
but left whole

½ teaspoon salt

½ teaspoon freshly ground
black pepper

Huacatay, also known as Peruvian black mint, has
a very distinctive flavour and is the most emblematic
of the Peruvian herbs, used in several traditional dishes
as well as modern ones. It isn't easy to find fresh outside
Peru, although you can grow it at home from seed
(its Latin name is *Tagetes minuta*), but ready-made
huacatay paste is available from specialist suppliers
(see page 217). You can also make a substitute herb
paste at home by combining mint, coriander, tarragon
and basil in equal proportions. Where huacatay is
used in other recipes in the book I have suggested an
alternative fresh herb, but if you do manage to source
fresh huacatay, you will bring an extra authentic touch
of Peruvian flavour to your dish.

1 Place all the herbs, oil, garlic and seasoning in a blender
and blend to a smooth paste.

2 Cover tightly and refrigerate until required,
or store in the freezer.

Salsa Huancaína

HUANCAÍNA SAUCE

Makes 500g

75g Ají Amarillo chillies
(see page 82) or any
mild yellow chillies

1½ tablespoons olive oil

280g red onions, cut into
large dice

2 garlic cloves, peeled
but left whole

60ml double cream

40g queso fresco (see page 56)
or ricotta cheese

1 teaspoon fine sea salt

1 teaspoon freshly ground
black pepper

This is Peru's most famous sauce and can be used in many dishes, as well as making a delicious dip. It first rose to popularity as a quick starter, served over boiled potatoes and accompanied by Peruvian black Botija olives (see page 158), lettuce and boiled eggs, and has since become a classic throughout the country.

1 Cut the chillies in half lengthways and remove the veins and seeds, then cut the chillies into large pieces.

2 Heat the oil in a sauté pan over a medium heat and sauté the red onions, garlic cloves and chillies for 5 minutes or until soft and lightly browned. Drain off any excess oil from the mixture.

3 Transfer the sautéed mixture to a blender, add the remaining ingredients and blend until smooth.

4 Cover tightly and refrigerate until required, or store in the freezer.

Salsa Ocopa

OCOPA SAUCE

This sauce is traditionally served with boiled potatoes, but is also good with chips, cheese or bread.

Makes 250g

½ dried Ají Amarillo (see page 82) or dried jalapeño chilli

40ml olive oil

25g huacatay sprigs (see page 88) or 10g mint and 40g flat leaf parsley, leaves picked

1 garlic clove, peeled but left whole

40g salted peanuts

50g cream crackers

50ml cold water

1 teaspoon fine sea salt

1 Remove the seeds and veins from the dried chilli half.

2 Heat the oil in a sauté pan over a medium heat and sauté the herbs, chilli and garlic clove for 5 minutes until the garlic is soft and lightly browned.

3 Transfer the sautéed mixture to a blender, add the remaining ingredients and blend to a smooth paste.

4 Cover tightly and refrigerate until required, or store in the freezer.

Queso Fresco y Ají Amarillo

QUESO FRESCO AND YELLOW AJÍ PASTE

Serve this as a dip – it is especially good with Duck
Escabeche Causa (see page 134).

Makes 320g

100g queso fresco (see page 56)
or ricotta cheese, plus an extra
50g to serve
125g Yellow Ají Paste
(see page 84)
50ml olive oil
25ml cold water
1 teaspoon fine sea salt
1 teaspoon ground cumin

1 Place all the ingredients in a blender and blend to a
soft paste.

2 Cover tightly and refrigerate until required, or store
in the freezer. Serve with extra queso fresco on top.

Uchucuta de Maní

PEANUT UCHUCUTA

This sauce is best suited to grilled meat or chicken skewers.
I also like to serve it with the Short Ribs Anticucho (see page 166).

Makes 240g

40g Ají Amarillo chillies
(see page 82) or any
mild-medium hot orange
or yellow chillies

75g salted peanuts, plus an
extra 10g crushed salted
peanuts to serve

25g queso fresco (see page 56)
or ricotta cheese

20g red onion, roughly chopped

2 garlic cloves, peeled
but left whole

handful of flat leaf parsley
leaves

handful of coriander leaves

75ml olive oil

1 teaspoon fine sea salt

½ teaspoon freshly ground
black pepper

1 Cut the chillies in half lengthways and remove the veins and seeds, then roughly chop.

2 Place in a blender, add all the remaining ingredients and blend until just combined.

3 Serve immediately sprinkled with crushed peanuts, or cover tightly and refrigerate until required.

Tiger's Milk, Chilli Pastes & Sauces

Salsa Criolla

SALSA CRIOLLA

Makes 150g

100g red onion
35g Ají Limo chilli (see page 83) or
any mild red or yellow chillies
1 teaspoon fine sea salt
½ tablespoon freshly squeezed
lime juice
1 tablespoon white wine
vinegar
1 tablespoon rapeseed or
olive oil
pinch of freshly ground black
pepper
a few coriander leaves

1 Chop the onion into thin slices, then leave to soak in cold water for 10 minutes.

2 Meanwhile, cut the chilli in half lengthways and remove the veins and seeds, then cut into thin slices.

3 Make a vinaigrette by adding the salt, lime juice and vinegar to a non-reactive bowl and whisk well until the salt has completely dissolved. Add the oil and black pepper and whisk until well combined.

4 Drain the onion and add to the vinaigrette with the chillies and coriander, then serve immediately.

Uchucuta de Palta

AVOCADO DIP

Serves 2

1 ripe avocado
2 tablespoons freshly squeezed
lime juice
fine sea salt and freshly ground
black pepper

1 Cut the avocado in half and remove the stone. Scoop out the avocado flesh into a blender or food processor, add the lime juice and blend until smooth. Transfer to a small serving bowl.

2 Season to taste with salt and pepper, then serve immediately.

Crema de Queso Fresco y Huacatay

QUESO FRESCO AND HUACATAY HERB CREAM

Serves 4

25ml full-fat milk
75ml double cream
120g queso fresco (see page 56)
or ricotta cheese
2 tablespoons finely chopped
white onion
½ teaspoon fine sea salt
1 tablespoon huacatay leaves
(see page 88) or coriander,
finely chopped (optional)

1 Heat the milk and 25ml cream together in a saucepan until warm, but do not let it boil.

2 Transfer to a blender, add the remaining cream, then add the rest of the ingredients and blend to a smooth, creamy mixture. Serve at room temperature.

Cactus fruit (or red tuna)

Aloe vera leaf

Cherimoya

Lúcuma

Huacatay leaf

Purple corn

CEVICHES, TIRADITOS & CAUSAS

Stories abound about the origins of ceviche and its name. Historians say that the Incas used tumbo fruit, a member of the Passiflora genus similar to passion fruit, or chicha (a corn 'beer' – see page 179) to marinate fish. There are also documents from the 16th century that describe the native coastal population preparing and eating raw fish using only salt and chilli. Later, with the arrival of the Spanish, lemon and onions were added to the preparation, giving the ceviche that we know today.

Among the many different accounts of where the name 'ceviche' came from, there are two that are the most plausible to Peruvians. Sivinche is a city in Arequipa, and in 1867, a recipe for marinated prawns was published in the Arequipan cookbook The Peruvian Table named 'sivinche'. The other likely derivation is from the Quechua word siwichi, meaning fresh fish.

Nowadays, ceviche is the dish most closely identified with Peruvian cuisine. It embodies the whole country's culinary character, and evokes a sense of national pride. Every family and restaurant has its own recipe.

In the past, people would marinate ceviche for many hours, but modern Peruvian cuisine has adopted the method developed by Pedro Solari in the 1930s of preparing the ceviche à la minute. He is credited by other masters of ceviche such as Javier Wong and Gastón Acurio as being the father of the modern ceviche.

More than just a dish, ceviche – or cebiche as it is called in Peru – represents a concept. There are only two central rules to making a perfect Peruvian ceviche: the use of fresh ingredients and the preparation minutes before serving. The cevicherías – restaurants that serve ceviche – are open only for lunch in Peru, upholding the old, traditional view that only in the morning are the fish truly fresh!

Ceviche de Corvina, Palta y Cebolla Morada

SEA BASS, AVOCADO AND RED ONION CEVICHE

The perfect ceviche requires the right balance between salt, acidity and spiciness: not too sour, and not too salty. An important trick is NEVER to squeeze the limes and lemons completely, otherwise it will turn bitter. Another important rule: NEVER let the ceviche marinate for more than 2 minutes before serving.

Serves 4

1 recipe quantity of Tiger's Milk Complete Recipe, made using 2 tablespoons Tiger's Milk Base and 30g sea bass fillet (see page 75)

400g very fresh skinless sea bass fillet, chilled

1 avocado

1 red onion, finely sliced

1 Ají Limo chilli (see page 83), jalapeño chilli or other mild red chilli, sliced, to garnish (optional)

fine sea salt

1 Follow the method on page 75 to prepare the Tiger's Milk. Cover and chill in the refrigerator.

2 Cut the sea bass into 2cm cubes.

3 Cut the avocado in half and remove the stone, then peel the avocado halves and cut into bite-sized chunks.

4 Place the sea bass and avocado cubes in serving bowls or on a serving platter. Pour just enough of the Tiger's Milk over but do not drown the fish.

5 Garnish the ceviche with red onion slices and the chilli slices if using, and serve immediately seasoned with fine sea salt to taste if necessary.

Ceviche de Conchas y Tomates

SCALLOPS AND TOMATOES

The sweet-acidic taste of the tomatoes is a perfect partner for
the scallops in this recipe, and the tomato flavoured Tiger's Milk
will give a final sweet-spicy touch to this delicate dish.

Serves 4

250g cherry tomatoes

1 recipe quantity of Tiger's Milk
Complete Recipe, but prepared
using 120ml lime juice and
2 tablespoons Tiger's Milk Base
(see page 75)

300g very fresh scallops,
shelled and cleaned

fine sea salt

coriander flowers (if available)
or leaves, to garnish

1 To skin the tomatoes, bring a saucepan of water to the boil.
Put some cold water and ice in a bowl. Score a small cross
in one end of each cherry tomato. Add the tomatoes to the
boiling water and leave for 10 seconds, then transfer to the
iced water but remove almost immediately. Using a paring
knife, remove the skin.

2 Put half of the tomatoes in a blender and blend for 2
minutes, then strain the juice through a fine-mesh sieve.

3 Follow the method on page 75 to prepare the Tiger's Milk,
then add 5 tablespoons of the tomato juice to the blender with
the other ingredients and blend for 3 minutes. Pass through a
fine-mesh sieve and adjust the seasoning adding more salt if
necessary. Cover and set aside in the refrigerator.

4 Cut the scallops in half.

5 Mix the reserved tomatoes with the Tiger's Milk mixture,
then spoon into a serving dish and arrange the scallops
on top.

6 Garnish the scallops and tomatoes with coriander flowers,
if available, or leaves and serve immediately.

Ceviche de Salmón, Ají Amarillo y Cancha

SALMON CEVICHE WITH YELLOW AJÍ AND CANCHA CORN

The addition of cancha corn kernels (see page 18) to ceviches is very common in Peru, but it is an optional ingredient that is usually served separately. We Peruvians love the crunchy texture combined with the tender fish and the spiciness of the aji. For us, it is the most satisfying comfort food!

Serves 4

1 recipe quantity of Tiger's Milk Complete Recipe (see page 75)
5 tablespoons Yellow Ají Paste (see page 84)
150g cooked cancha corn kernels (see page 18)
400g very fresh skinless salmon fillet, pin-boned
fine sea salt
chives, dill and green mustard leaves, roughly chopped, to garnish

1 Put the Tiger's Milk in a blender with the Yellow Ají Paste and blend for 3 minutes. Pass through a fine-mesh sieve and adjust the seasoning adding more salt if necessary. Cover and set aside in the refrigerator.

2 Crush the cooked corn kernels with a mallet, then set aside for the garnish.

3 Cut the salmon into 2cm cubes.

4 Place the salmon cubes in a deep plate or a wide bowl and pour the Tiger's Milk mixture over the salmon to dress it. Garnish with the crushed corn kernels and herbs.

Ceviche Caliente de Trucha y Rocoto

TROUT AND ROCOTO HOT CEVICHE

Most people think that ceviche must be eaten cold. However, hot ceviches are also delicious and don't involve much more preparation. You can also adapt other cold ceviche recipes by warming the fish and the Tiger's Milk before serving.

Serves 4

1 recipe quantity of Tiger's Milk Complete Recipe (see page 75)
2 teaspoons Ají Rocoto Paste (see page 86)
3 sweetcorn husks (optional)
150g skinless trout fillet, pin-boned
1 teaspoon olive oil
fine sea salt

1 Put the Tiger's Milk in a blender, add the Ají Rocoto Paste and blend for 3 minutes. Pass through a fine-mesh sieve and adjust the seasoning adding more salt if necessary. Cover and set aside in the refrigerator.

2 Char the sweetcorn husks, if using, over a gas flame on the hob, then place in the base of a serving bowl.

3 Heat the Tiger's Milk mixture in a saucepan over a gentle heat for 5 minutes.

4 Meanwhile, cut the trout into large chunks and season with 1 teaspoon salt. Heat the oil in a sauté pan over a high heat and sear the trout on all sides.

5 Arrange the trout on top of the sweetcorn husks, or in a serving bowl, and pour the hot Tiger's Milk over the top. Serve immediately.

Ceviche de Mero y Rocoto

GROUPER AND CHILI CEVICHE

This is a classic combination that can be made with various types of fish and different chillies. Once you learn the principles of making ceviche with fresh fish and Tiger's Milk you can substitute whatever ingredients are available to you and create your own unique version.

Serves 4

1 recipe quantity of Tiger's Milk
Complete Recipe, made using
2 tablespoons Tiger's Milk Base
(see page 75)
4 tablespoons Ají Rocoto Paste
(see page 86)
400g very fresh skinless
grouper fillet, pin-boned and
cut into 2cm cubes
fine sea salt

TO GARNISH
1 red onion, finely sliced
oxalis leaves, to garnish
(optional)

1 Put the Tiger's Milk in a blender with the Ají Rocoto Paste and blend for 3 minutes. Pass through a fine-mesh sieve and adjust the seasoning adding more salt if necessary.

2 Spoon the Tiger's Milk mixture into a shallow serving bowl and arrange the grouper cubes on top.

3 Garnish with the red onion slices and the oxalis leaves, if available.

Zapallo Italiano

COURGETTE AND BABY CARROT CEVICHE

This is a vegetarian version of a classic ceviche. It can be served either as a starter or as an accompaniment for other dishes. You can also be creative and use other vegetables, such as celery or peppers, and adapt the Tiger's Milk recipe to change the colour and spiciness.

Serves 4

1 recipe quantity of Tiger's Milk Complete Recipe, but prepared using 2 tablespoons Tiger's Milk Base (see page 75)

4 tablespoons Ají Rocoto Paste (see page 86)

4 courgettes

20 baby carrots

fine sea salt

Virgilio's Tip

You can omit the fish in the Tiger's Milk to make this recipe vegetarian.

1 Add the Tiger's Milk to the blender with the Ají Rocoto Paste and blend for 3 minutes. Pass through a fine-mesh sieve and adjust the seasoning adding more salt if necessary. Cover and set aside in the refrigerator.

2 Using a vegetable peeler, shave the courgettes lengthways, then set aside.

3 Peel the carrots and cut them in half crossways. Cook under a medium-high grill, turning frequently, until well browned.

4 Mix the top halves of the grilled carrots and courgette shavings with the Tiger's Milk mixture in a bowl.

5 Transfer to a serving bowl and garnish with the tips of the grilled baby carrots.

Ceviche de Maiz Bebé

BABY CORN CEVICHE

Serves 4

1 recipe quantity of Tiger's Milk
Complete Recipe (see page 75)
2 teaspoons Yellow Ají Paste
(see page 84)
4 sweetcorn husks (optional)
16 baby corn cobs
fine sea salt

Virgilio's Tip
*You can omit the fish in
the Tiger's Milk to make this
recipe vegetarian.*

1 Add the Tiger's Milk to a blender with the Yellow Ají Paste and blend for 3 minutes. Pass through a fine-mesh sieve and adjust the seasoning adding more salt if necessary. Cover and set aside in the refrigerator.

2 Char the sweetcorn husks, if using, over a gas flame on the hob, then place in the base of a serving bowl.

3 Cook the baby corn under a medium-high grill, turning frequently, until well browned.

4 Place the baby corn on top of the sweetcorn husks or in a serving bowl and pour over the Tiger's Milk. Serve immediately.

Ceviche de Dos Quinuas y Palta

TWO QUINOAS AND AVOCADO CEVICHE

Serves 4

1 recipe quantity of Tiger's Milk
Complete Recipe (see page 75)
75ml passion fruit juice
200g red quinoa
100g white quinoa
2 avocados
½ tablespoon freshly squeezed
lime juice
2 tablespoons extra virgin
olive oil
fine sea salt

Virgilio's Tip
*You can omit the fish in
the Tiger's Milk to make this
recipe vegetarian.*

1 Add the Tiger's Milk to a blender with the passion fruit juice and blend for 3 minutes. Pass through a fine-mesh sieve and adjust the seasoning adding more salt if necessary. Cover and set aside in the refrigerator.

2 Rinse the 2 types of quinoa separately in cold running water until the water runs clear, then drain.

3 Place each quinoa in a separate saucepan with tight-fitting lids and add water to cover by 5cm. Cover with the lid and bring to the boil over a medium heat. Stir, re-cover and reduce the heat to low. Cook for about 15 minutes – the quinoa is ready when you can see a little ring on the outside of the grain and it is soft. Rinse in cold water, then drain and set aside.

4 Cut the avocados in half and remove the stones, then peel the avocado halves. Place in a blender with the lime juice, a pinch of salt and the olive oil and blend until creamy.

5 Mix the quinoas with the Tiger's Milk mixture.

6 Spoon the creamy avocado into a serving bowl and top with the quinoa mixture. Serve immediately.

The word *tiradito* is probably derived from the Spanish '*estiradito*', meaning 'stretched', and consists of thin, sashimi-style strips of fish. It is the result of the influence of Japanese immigrants on Peruvian cuisine, their superior skill with the kitchen knife and cooking techniques having been applied to local ingredients. Tiradito can be classified as a subcategory of ceviche, and there are many contemporary versions that bring an extra flavour dimension to the classic dish. As a child, I remember after a day's fishing on the coast how the fish was prepared in this way – the fresh fish cut into thin slices and dressed with lime juice, salt and Ají (chilli) slices, and nothing else. This simple, delicate yet iconic Peruvian dish evokes a childhood memory I will always treasure.

Tiradito de Corvina y Cilantro

SEA BASS AND CORIANDER TIRADITO

Serves 4

1 recipe quantity of Tiger's Milk Complete Recipe (see page 75)

1 tablespoon puréed coriander

caster sugar, to taste

400g very fresh skinless sea bass or sole fillet, pin-boned

fine sea salt

2 tablespoons borage flowers, to garnish (optional)

1 Add the Tiger's Milk to a blender with the puréed coriander and blend. Pass through a fine-mesh sieve and adjust the seasoning with fine sea salt and sugar to taste. Cover and set aside in the refrigerator for 5 minutes.

2 Using a sharp knife, cut the fish into thin slices on the diagonal, sashimi style, and arrange on chilled serving plates.

3 Dress with the Tiger's Milk mixture, then garnish with borage flowers, if available. Serve immediately.

Tiradito de Pez Pampanito, Chía y Ají Amarillo

RED SNAPPER, CHIA AND YELLOW AJÍ TIRADITO

The gel-like texture of hydrated chia (see page 26) adds an interesting element to this dish. It has a neutral flavour, but adds a beautiful and extra healthy element to this Tiradito. If you have time, you can create modern patterns using both Tiger's Milk and chia gel before serving it.

Serves 4

2 teaspoons fresh turmeric root, peeled and grated

150ml boiling water

1 tablespoon chia seeds (see page 26)

1 recipe quantity of Tiger's Milk Complete Recipe but prepared using 2 tablespoons Tiger's Milk Base (see page 75)

2 tablespoons Yellow Ají Paste (see page 84)

400g very fresh skinless red snapper fillet, pin-boned

fine sea salt

nasturtium petals and leaves, to garnish (optional)

1 Cook the turmeric in the boiling water in a small saucepan for 20 minutes.

2 Remove from the heat and leave to cool. Add the chia seeds and leave to hydrate until it turns into a thin, jelly-like consistency. Set aside.

3 Add the Tiger's Milk to a blender with the Yellow Ají Paste and blend for 3 minutes. Pass through a fine-mesh sieve and adjust the seasoning adding more salt if necesssary. Cover and set aside in the refrigerator for 5 minutes.

4 Using a sharp knife, cut the red snapper into thin slices on the diagonal, sashimi style, and arrange on a chilled serving platter.

5 Dress with the Tiger's Milk mixture and the turmeric chia jelly, then garnish with nasturtium petals and leaves, if available. Serve immediately.

Tiradito de Salmón e Hinojo Verde

SALMON AND FENNEL TIRADITO

Fennel has a wonderful crunchy texture and a gentle anise flavour. The bulb and the leaves are both edible and are equally delicious raw or cooked. Here, I've added fresh, raw fennel to complement the salmon.

Serves 4

1 recipe quantity of Tiger's Milk Complete Recipe but prepared using 2 tablespoons Tiger's Milk Base (see page 75)

2 teaspoons Ají Rocoto Paste (see page 87)

300g very fresh skinless salmon fillet, pin-boned

¼ fennel bulb, trimmed and thinly sliced, fronds reserved

fine sea salt

1 Add the Tiger's Milk to the blender, with the Rocoto Ají Paste and blend for 3 minutes. Pass through a fine-mesh sieve and adjust the seasoning adding more salt if necessary. Cover and refrigerate for 5 minutes.

2 Using a sharp knife, cut the salmon into thin slices on the diagonal, sashimi style, and arrange on a chilled serving platter.

3 Dress with the Tiger's Milk and fennel fronds, then serve.

Tiradito de Zanahoria Roja Asada, Berenjena y Cebolla Perla

GRILLED RED CARROT, AUBERGINE AND PEARL ONIONS

Serves 4

2 red carrots

2 aubergines

300g spinach leaves

1 recipe quantity of Tiger's Milk Complete Recipe (see page 75)

2 teaspoons olive oil

200g baby onions, peeled but left whole

1 Using a vegetable peeler, peel the carrots, then run the peeler down the length of each carrot to make shavings. Repeat with the unpeeled aubergines.

2 Place the spinach in a blender and blend to a purée, adding a little water if necessary. Strain off any excess liquid.

3 Add the Tiger's Milk to a blender with the puréed spinach, then blend. Pass through a fine-mesh sieve. Cover and refrigerate for 5 minutes.

4 Heat a sauté pan, add 1 teaspoon olive oil and gently fry the aubergine shavings on both sides until golden.

5 Meanwhile, heat another sauté pan, add the remaining teaspoon of olive oil and cook the carrot shavings and baby onions, tossing frequently, until they are all lightly golden.

6 Place the Tiger's Milk mixture on a serving platter, top with the vegetable shavings and serve immediately.

Tiradito de Lenguado con Dos Leches de Tigre

SOLE TIRADITO WITH RED AND YELLOW TIGER'S MILK

Serves 4

400g very fresh skinless sole fillet, pin-boned
¼ teaspoon sea salt flakes
oxalis leaves, to garnish (optional)

RED AJÍ TIGER'S MILK

1 recipe quantity of Tiger's Milk Complete Recipe (see page 75)
1 tablespoon Ají Rocoto Paste (see page 87)
sugar, to taste

YELLOW AJÍ TIGER'S MILK

1 quantity of Tiger's Milk Complete Recipe (see page 75)
1 tablespoon Yellow Ají Paste (see page 84)
fine sea salt

1 To make the Red Ají Tiger's Milk, follow the method on page 75 to prepare the Tiger's Milk but add the Ají Rocoto Paste to the blender and blend for 3 minutes. Pass through a fine-mesh sieve and adjust the seasoning adding more salt and sugar to taste. Cover and refrigerate for 5 minutes.

2 Repeat for the Yellow Ají Tiger's Milk but using the Yellow Ají Paste instead of the Ají Rocoto Paste.

3 Using a sharp knife, cut the sole fillet into thin slices on the diagonal, sashimi style, and arrange on a chilled serving platter.

4 Dress with the 2 types of Tiger's Milk and sprinkle with sea salt flakes, then garnish with oxalis leaves, if available. Serve immediately.

Tiradito de Lomo de Ternera y Quinua Negra

VEAL LOIN AND BLACK QUINOA TIRADITO

Serves 4

1 recipe quantity of Tiger's Milk Complete Recipe but prepared using 2 tablespoons Tiger's Milk Base (see page 75)

5 tablespoons Ají Rocoto Paste (see page 87)

sugar, to taste

150g mayonnaise (see page 131 for homemade)

2 tablespoons beetroot juice

ice cubes

1 teaspoon groundnut oil

400g veal loin

150g black quinoa

2 teaspoons beetroot powder (see Virgilio's Tip)

fine sea salt

Virgilio's Tip
You will find beetroot powder in health food stores or online from health food suppliers.

1 Add the Tiger's Milk to a blender with the Ají Rocoto Paste and blend for 3 minutes. Pass through a fine-mesh sieve and adjust the seasoning adding more salt and sugar to taste. Cover and set aside in the refrigerator.

2 Mix the mayonnaise with the beetroot juice. Cover and set aside in the refrigerator.

3 Prepare a bowl with water and add ice cubes. Heat the groundnut oil in a large frying pan over a high heat, add the veal loin and sear on all sides, cooking for 1 minute on each side.

4 Immerse the seared meat in the iced water to cool it instantly. Transfer to kitchen paper and pat dry. Set aside.

5 Rinse the quinoa in cold running water until the water runs clear, then drain.

6 Place the quinoa in a saucepan with a tight-fitting lid and add water to cover by 5cm. Cover with the lid and bring to the boil over a medium heat. Stir, re-cover and reduce the heat to low. Cook for about 15 minutes – the quinoa is ready when you can see a little ring on the outside of the grain and it is soft. Rinse in cold water, then drain.

7 Dress the quinoa with some of the Tiger's Milk mixture.

8 Using a sharp knife, cut the veal on the diagonal into 1cm slices – it will be rare in the centre. Arrange on a flat serving platter.

9 Garnish the veal with the dressed quinoa and add more Tiger's Milk mixture and some dots of the beetroot mayonnaise, then sprinkle with the beetroot powder.

'Causa' comes from the word 'causay' or 'kausay' in the Quechua language, meaning 'nourishment', and as with all Peruvian dishes causas have many stories and traditions associated with them. Pre-Hispanic Andean people prepared mashed potatoes with chilli to make causa, a kind of savoury cake. This causay was then enhanced during the colonial period with the addition of new ingredients, namely avocados, fish and olives. The Republican version of the dish, causa limeña, introduced boiled eggs to the colonial combination, and was sometimes prepared with chicken instead of fish. That recipe is associated with a 'political cause', as the dish was served to soldiers during the celebration of Independence Day. Causas can be served as a family-sized cold pie to share, or in small, bite-sized gnocchi shapes. It can be also formed into cubes and other shapes, such as rectangles – in fact, contemporary Peruvian cuisine can't stop inventing new ways to present this simple yet exciting dish!

Masa de Causa

CAUSA DOUGH

Makes about 1kg

1kg blue potatoes (for purple dough) or King Edward potatoes (for yellow dough), skins on, washed and cut into quarters

50ml rapeseed oil

5 tablespoons Yellow Ají Paste (see page 84)

50ml freshly squeezed lime juice

fine sea salt and freshly ground black pepper

1 Place the potatoes in a saucepan, cover with water and add 2 teaspoons salt.

2 Bring to the boil and cook for about 20 minutes or until tender. Drain and set aside until cool enough to handle.

3 Peel the potatoes, then pass through a potato ricer or mash them.

4 Beat in the rapeseed oil, Yellow Ají paste, lime juice and salt and pepper to taste.

5 Use as directed in your chosen recipe (see pages 131–8).

Causa Tradicional de Pollo, Palta y Huevo

TRADITIONAL CHICKEN, AVOCADO AND EGG CAUSA

Serves 6

1 boneless, skinless
chicken breast
1 teaspoon fine sea salt
1 recipe quantity of Causa
Dough (see page 129)

HOMEMADE MAYONNAISE

4 organic or free-range
egg yolks
1 tablespoon white wine
vinegar
200ml vegetable oil
1–2 teaspoons fine sea salt
1 teaspoon freshly ground
black pepper

TO GARNISH

2 hard-boiled eggs, shelled and
chopped
1 avocado, stoned, peeled
and cut into strips

1 To make the mayonnaise, place the egg yolks in a large, clean bowl. Lay a damp cloth under the base of the bowl to hold it securely in place. Add the vinegar to the egg yolks and, using a large balloon whisk, whisk to blend. Add a very small amount of the oil and whisk again until it is well blended. Add a little more oil and whisk again. Continue adding the oil, whisking thoroughly between each addition, until the sauce emulsifies and thickens, which will take a few minutes. Stop adding the oil when the mayonnaise has reached the desired consistency. Season with the salt and pepper to taste and blend well. Cover and set aside in the refrigerator.

2 Cook the chicken breast in boiling water with the 1 teaspoon salt for about 20 minutes or until cooked through and tender. Drain and leave to cool, then shred and mix with the mayonnaise. Cover and set aside in the refrigerator.

3 Line the base and sides of a baking dish with clingfilm.

4 Spread half the Causa Dough over the base of the lined dish to form a smooth, even layer. Spread the chicken and mayonnaise mixture over the Causa Dough and then spread the remaining Causa Dough evenly over the filling. Press down gently to firm up, then cover and chill thoroughly – for at least 1 hour.

5 Garnish the dish decoratively with the chopped hard-boiled eggs and avocado strips.

Causa de Papa Amarilla, Caballa y Palta

YELLOW CAUSA WITH CURED MACKEREL AND AVOCADO

Serves 4

1 recipe quantity of Causa
Dough made with olive oil
instead of rapeseed oil
(see page 129)

CURED MACKEREL
250g sea salt flakes
100g caster sugar
1½ teaspoons crushed
pink peppercorns
1 teaspoon finely grated
orange zest
200g mackerel, gutted

TO GARNISH
red onion slices
watercress

1 To prepare the cured mackerel, combine the salt, sugar, pink peppercorns and orange zest in a large, deep tray. Place the mackerel on the tray and cover with the dry cure mixture. Cover the tray and refrigerate for 30 minutes.

2 Remove the fish from the tray and wash off the dry cure. Pat the fish dry with kitchen paper, then cut it in half or into thin slices. Cover and set aside in the refrigerator.

3 Line the base and sides of a baking dish with clingfilm.

4 Spread the Causa Dough over the base of the lined dish to form a smooth, even layer. Press down gently to firm up, then cover and chill thoroughly – for at least 1 hour.

5 When ready to serve, turn the dish upside down to remove the causa and carefully discard the clingfilm. Cut the causa into rectangles about 11 x 4cm and place on serving plates. Arrange the cured mackerel on the top of the causa, and garnish with the red onion slices and watercress.

Causa de Escabeche de Pato

DUCK ESCABECHE CAUSA

Serves 6

2 tablespoons olive oil,
plus extra if needed

2 boneless duck breasts,
skinned

1 onion, halved and cut into
thin half-moon slices

2 garlic cloves, very finely
chopped

1 tablespoon deveined,
deseeded and crumbled dried
Ají Panca chilli (see page 83) or
1 tablespoon Ají Panca Paste
(see page 84)

1 tablespoon soft dark
brown sugar

1 teaspoon ground cumin

1 teaspoon paprika

3 teaspoons fine sea salt

125ml chicken stock,
plus extra if needed

175ml white wine

4 tablespoons white wine
vinegar

1 bay leaf

2 tablespoons capers

400g spinach leaves

1 recipe quantity of Causa
Dough made with olive oil
instead of rapeseed oil (see
page 129)

1 Heat 1 tablespoon of the olive oil in a heavy-based frying pan over a medium-high heat.

2 Add the duck breasts and brown on both sides. Remove to a plate.

3 Add the onion, garlic, chilli, sugar, cumin, paprika and salt to the pan, with another tablespoon of olive oil if necessary, and cook at a medium-low heat, stirring occasionally, for about 8 minutes until the onion is soft and fragrant.

4 Return the duck breasts to the pan, nestling the pieces in with the onion and spices, then add the stock, wine, vinegar and bay leaf. Add a little more stock if there is not enough liquid, but you do not need to completely cover the duck with it. Cover the pan and cook over a low heat for about 20 minutes, then uncover.

5 Add the capers and simmer for about a further 5 minutes.

6 Discard the bay leaf. Lift the duck breasts out and cut into slices. Strain the sauce through a sieve, reserving the solids, and set aside.

7 Place the spinach in a blender and blend to a purée, then mix thoroughly with the Causa Dough until the mixture is an even colour.

8 Line the base and sides of a baking dish with clingfilm.

9 Spread half the spinach Causa Dough over the base of the lined dish to form a smooth, even layer. Arrange three-quarters of the duck slices evenly over the Causa Dough. Spread the remaining Causa Dough evenly over the filling. Press down gently to firm up.

10 Tear the remaining duck into pieces and garnish, then serve in the dish with the sauce poured on top and the reserved onion and chilli scattered over it.

Causa de Calamar, Papa Morada y Cebolla Encurtida

SQUID AND BLUE POTATO CAUSA WITH PICKLED ONION

Serves 4

1 quantity of Causa Dough
made with blue potatoes
(see pages 129 and 14)
2 squid, cleaned
rapeseed oil, for shallow-frying
1 teaspoon fine sea salt
edible flowers and herbs,
to garnish (optional)

PICKLED ONION

1 large onion, finely sliced
110ml red wine vinegar
1 tablespoon clear honey
2 tablespoons olive oil
1 tablespoon finely chopped
coriander
1 teaspoon fine sea salt
½ teaspoon freshly ground
black pepper

1 To prepare the pickled onion, combine all the ingredients in a non-reactive bowl. Cover and leave to marinate at room temperature for 20 minutes.

2 Line the base and sides of a baking dish with clingfilm.

3 Spread the Causa Dough over the base of the lined dish to form a smooth, even layer. Press down gently to firm up. Set aside.

4 Cut each squid body in half lengthways. Using a sharp knife, score the insides in a criss-cross pattern.

5 Heat a sauté pan over a high heat. Add enough oil to coat the base of pan. Season the squid with the salt, add to the pan and sauté until lightly browned. The squid will naturally form into rolls. Remove and cut into 3cm pieces.

6 Turn the dish upside down to remove the Causa Dough and carefully discard the clingfilm. Cut the causa into large cubes, about 3cm square, and place on a serving platter. Place the warm sautéed squid on top and garnish with the pickled onion, and edible flowers and herbs, if desired.

Causa de Pulpo y Pimientos del Piquillo

OCTOPUS AND PIQUILLO CAUSA

Serves 4

2kg cleaned octopus (without the head), washed
(see step 2, page 158)
2 white onions, 1 roughly chopped and 1 thinly sliced
2 celery sticks, 1 roughly chopped and 1 thinly sliced
1 carrot, roughly chopped
120g drained piquillo peppers from a jar, plus extra, chopped, to garnish
1 quantity of Causa Dough (see page 129)
1 tablespoon olive oil (optional)
fine sea salt

TO GARNISH
5 teaspoons Huancaína Sauce (see page 89)
herbs

1 Bring a deep saucepan of water to the boil, add the octopus, the roughly chopped onion and celery, the carrot and 1 teaspoon salt and cook for about 1 hour or until the octopus is tender. Test after 40 minutes by piercing the octopus with a fork where the tentacles meet its body – if the fork goes through fairly easily, it's ready. If it still feels firm, reduce the heat and leave until fork tender.

2 Drain the octopus and leave to cool, then slice it into bite-sized chunks and place in a bowl. Add the sliced onion and celery to the octopus and mix well, then cover and chill in the refrigerator.

3 Pat the piquillo peppers dry with kitchen paper, then place in a blender and blend to a purée. Set aside.

4 Mix the piquillo purée thoroughly with the Causa Dough until the mixture is an even colour.

5 Line the base and sides of a baking dish with clingfilm.

6 Spread the Causa Dough over the base of the lined dish to form a smooth, even layer. Press down gently to firm up and set aside.

7 Heat the oil in a sauté pan over a high heat and sear the cooked octopus on the outside. Alternatively, place under a high grill until browned. Season to taste with salt.

8 Turn the dsh upside down to remove the Causa Dough and carefully discard the clingfilm. Cut the causa into rectangles, about 11 x 4cm and arrange on a serving dish. Place the octopus pieces on top and garnish with the chopped piquillo peppers, the Huancaína Sauce and herbs, if desired.

**VEGETARIAN
MAIN COURSES**

Lechugas Salteadas, 'Tocino Vegetal' y Yogurt

SAUTÉED LETTUCE, 'VEGETARIAN BACON' AND YOGURT

This is a delicious and simple dish that can be served as a salad or a side dish (in which case without the yogurt dressing). We are used to Little Gem leaves being served fresh in salads, but if you gently sauté the leaves in a little oil you will have a surprise - they take on a whole new flavour. In this dish I've used potatoes with red or slightly purple flesh to make the crisps that look like bacon strips, adding a fun touch to the dish!

Serves 4

240ml natural yogurt
2 teaspoons freshly squeezed lemon juice
1 teaspoon Dijon mustard
1 teaspoon chopped flat leaf parsley
1 teaspoon chopped chives
2 tablespoons olive oil
140g Little Gem lettuce, washed, dried and chopped
20g sea lettuce or dried seaweed
1 teaspoon fine sea salt
freshly ground black pepper

TO SERVE
15g Blue Potato Crisps
(see page 14)
75g Sweet Potato Crisps
(see page 14)

1 Whisk the yogurt and lemon juice together in a small bowl until smooth. Stir in the mustard, parsley and chives. Cover and refrigerate until ready to serve.

2 Heat the olive oil in a sauté pan and sauté the Little Gem lettuce and sea lettuce or dried seaweed over a medium-high heat for 1 minute. Add the salt and pepper to taste.

3 Place 5 tablespoons of the dressing in the base of a serving dish, put the Little Gem lettuce on top and garnish with the Blue Potato Crisps and the Sweet Potato Crisps.

Puré de Papas, Coles de Bruselas y Vainitas con Flores Comestibles

MASHED POTATOES, BRUSSELS SPROUTS AND GREEN BEANS WITH EDIBLE FLOWERS

You will not believe how many flowers in your garden are edible: nasturtiums, orange blossom, pea flowers, the flowers from common herbs, such as coriander, basil, chives, dill, fennel, sage and borage, garlic and onion flowers, and even decorative flowers such as lavender and rose. Here, I've taken my favourite edible flowers and used them to decorate this beautiful dish.

Serves 4

800g King Edward potatoes, peeled and cut into quarters

70ml milk

40g butter, diced

1 tablespoon chopped flat leaf parsley

2 tablespoons olive oil

2 teaspoons crushed garlic

¼ white onion, chopped

450g Brussels sprouts, trimmed

garlic powder, to taste

200g green beans, topped and tailed and each split lengthways

2 tablespoons edible flowers and young herbs

fine sea salt and freshly ground black pepper

1 Cook the potatoes in a saucepan of salted boiling water for about 20 minutes until fork tender but not falling apart.

2 Meanwhile, in another saucepan, heat the milk.

3 Drain the potatoes well and return to the hot pan over a low heat. Roughly mash the potatoes. Add the butter and hot milk to the mashed potatoes and mix with a spoon until fluffy. Season to taste with salt and pepper. Add the chopped parsley, then set aside.

4 Heat 1 tablespoon of the olive oil in a cast-iron frying pan over a medium heat until the oil shimmers. Add the garlic and cook, stirring frequently, for about 3 minutes until golden brown and fragrant. Add the onion and cook, again stirring frequently, for about 5 minutes until soft.

5 Add the Brussels sprouts to the pan and cook them, without stirring, for 5–7 minutes until the undersides turn golden brown. Stir to turn the sprouts over and cook the other sides for a further 5–7 minutes until golden brown. Season with salt and pepper, and garlic powder. Remove from the pan.

6 Repeat the same process with the green beans, using the remaining tablespoon of olive oil.

7 To serve, on a serving platter, form one half of a circle with half the mashed potatoes, covering them with the flowers and herbs. Form the other half of a circle with the cooked Brussels sprouts, covering them with the green beans.

Arroz Chaufa Vegetal

VEGETABLE 'CHAUFA' RICE

The word 'chaufa' is derived from the Chinese and means 'eating rice'. This is Chinese-style fried rice with a Peruvian twist.

Serves 4

2 quantities of Rice with White Corn but without the corn (see page 67)

20g baby carrots, roughly chopped

4 tablespoons rapeseed oil

1 tablespoon peeled and very finely chopped fresh root ginger

1 tablespoon very finely chopped garlic

1 red pepper, chopped into bite-sized pieces

45g drained hearts of palm from a jar or can (see page 55), sliced into rings

40g cherry tomatoes, skinned

2 shallots, cut into quarters

250g baby radish

2 kale leaves

3 tablespoons soy sauce

1 tablespoon sesame oil

fine sea salt

TO GARNISH

2 Bahuaja (Brazil) nuts, shelled and grated

Huancaína Sauce (see page 89)

1 Follow the method on page 67 to prepare the rice but without using the corn. Set aside.

2 Parboil the carrots for 3 minutes, then remove and set aside.

3 Heat the rapeseed oil in a wok or large sauté pan over a medium-high heat and stir-fry the ginger and garlic for a few seconds.

4 Add the carrots, red pepper, hearts of palm, cherry tomatoes, shallots, radish and kale leaves and stir-fry for 5–7 minutes.

5 Add 2 tablespoons of the soy sauce and sauté for 1 minute.

6 Add the cooked rice, stir and then add the remaining tablespoon of soy sauce and the sesame oil. Season to taste with salt.

7 Garnish the rice with the grated nuts and drops of Huancaína Sauce.

Quinua con Colinabo y Cebolla Perla

QUINOA WITH KOHLRABI AND PEARL ONIONS

Quinoa is one of Peru's staple foods (see page 58) and is as healthy as it is versatile. Quinoa can be used as a substitute for rice and its texture will change when sautéed or fried. In this recipe I have used white quinoa, but you can use any variety. If available garnish with borage flowers, but feel free to use other edible flowers or your favourite seasonal herbs.

Serves 4

240g white quinoa

3 tablespoons olive oil

50g baby onions, peeled but left whole

100g trimmed purple kohlrabi, peeled and thinly sliced

20g capers

1cm piece of fresh root ginger, peeled and grated

handful of coriander and flat leaf parsley, chopped

fine sea salt and freshly ground black pepper

handful of borage flowers and young herbs, to garnish

1 Rinse the quinoa in cold running water until the water runs clear, then drain.

2 Place the quinoa in a saucepan with a tight-fitting lid and add water to cover by 5cm. Cover with the lid and bring to the boil over a medium heat. Stir, re-cover and reduce the heat to low. Cook for about 15 minutes – the quinoa is ready when you can see a little ring on the outside of the grain and it is soft. Rinse in cold water, then drain well.

3 Heat 1 tablespoon of the olive oil in a sauté pan and sauté the quinoa for 5 minutes. Set aside.

4 Heat another 1 tablespoon olive oil in a separate pan and sauté the onions until golden. Add the kohlrabi and capers.

5 Add the remaining tablespoon of olive oil to the first pan and sauté the grated ginger for 20 seconds. Add the sautéed quinoa and vegetables, and season with salt and pepper to taste, then stir in the chopped herbs. Serve garnished with the borage flowers and young herbs.

FISH & MEAT

Jalea

JALEA

Jalea is an ancient technique for preserving fish, developed by the Moche people who thrived in northern Peru almost 2,000 years ago. The fish was cut into pieces and dried in the sun before being grilled. Nowadays in Peru, *jalea* is mostly associated with a dish of small pieces of fish and seafood battered and deep-fried.

Serves 4

200g cleaned octopus tenacles, washed

200g cleaned squid, washed and cut into rings

200g skinless red snapper or sea bass fillets

110g plain flour or rice flour

450ml rapeseed oil

fine sea salt and freshly ground black pepper

TO GARNISH

5 tablespoons cored, deseeded and finely chopped red or orange pepper

¼ red onion, finely diced

cooked cancha corn kernels (see page 18), optional

coriander leaves from the flowering stem, to garnish (optional)

1 Place the octopus tentacles in a large bowl and rinse under cold running water until the water in the bowl is clear and the octopus skin feels clean, with no traces of grit.

2 Pat the octopus and squid rings dry with a clean tea towel. Cut the fish into cubes.

3 Place the fish and seafood in a bowl, season with salt and pepper and sprinkle the flour on top. Mix until well coated.

4 Transfer the fish and seafood in batches to a colander and shake off the excess flour.

5 Heat the rapeseed oil in a deep-fat fryer or in a deep, heavy-based saucepan over a medium heat to 180–190°C, or until a cube of bread browns in 30 seconds. Add the fish and seafood in batches and fry until golden. Transfer to a plate covered with kitchen paper.

6 Serve hot, garnished with the pepper, red onion, cancha corn and coriander leaves, if desired.

Rape al Ají Panca y Pasta de Quinua

AJÍ PANCA MONKFISH WITH TOASTED QUINOA PASTA

Serves 4

1 litre water
600g monkfish fillet
4 tablespoons Ají Panca Paste
(see page 85)
f2 tablespoons olive oil, plus
extra for drizzling
4 tablespoons Andean Herb
Chimichurri (see page 88)
ine sea salt
herbs of your choice, to garnish

TOASTED QUINOA
PASTA DOUGH

450g white quinoa (370g
for the pasta, plus extra
for dusting)
3 eggs
½ teaspoon fine sea salt
½ teaspoon extra virgin
olive oil

Virgilio's Tip

*You can prepare a larger
quantity of toasted quinoa flour
in advance and then store in an
airtight container in the freezer.
This way, you will keep it fresh
and avoid it turning rancid.*

1 To prepare toasted quinoa flour for the pasta (see Virgilio's Tip, opposite), preheat the oven to 110°C, Gas Mark ¼. Place the quinoa in a food processor and process to a fine flour.

2 Spread the freshly ground quinoa flour on a baking sheet and roast in the oven for 2 hours, stirring it every 30 minutes. Remove from the oven and leave to cool completely.

3 To make the pasta, mound the 370g toasted quinoa flour on a clean work surface. Make a well in the centre of the flour with steep sides. Break the eggs into the well, then add the salt and olive oil and gently mix into the eggs with a fork. Gradually incorporate the flour from the sides of the well into the egg mixture until a dough begins to form.

4 Using your hands or a dough (bench) scraper, continue working the dough until it comes together. If the dough is too dry, add a little water; if too wet or sticky, add a little flour.

5 Knead the dough for about 8–10 minutes, or until it becomes smooth and elastic. At this point, set the dough aside, cover it with clingfilm and leave it to rest for 15–20 minutes. You can store the dough in the refrigerator for up to 24 hours, but allow it to return to room temperature before rolling it out.

6 Divide the pasta dough evenly into 4 pieces. Keep each piece of dough covered with clingfilm or a clean tea towel while you work on each one in turn. Dust the dough, the rollers of a pasta machine or your rolling pin, your hands and the work surface with flour.

7 If using a pasta machine, flatten a dough piece between your hands or with a floured rolling pin until it forms a thick, oval disc. Dust the disc, the roller and your hands with additional flour. Flour a baking sheet to hold the rolled-out pasta.

8 With the pasta machine on its widest setting, pass the dough through the machine's rollers a few times until it is smooth. Fold the dough over and continue to pass through a few more times until the pasta is smooth again. Gradually reduce the setting width on the pasta machine, passing the dough through a few times at each setting. At the end, the pasta should look like thin lasagne. Place on the floured baking sheet.

9 If rolling the pasta by hand, sprinkle flour on the work surface and flatten a dough piece into a thick, oval disc with your hands. Sprinkle it with additional flour if necessary. Begin rolling out the dough with a floured rolling pin, working from the centre of the dough outwards, constantly moving the dough and lifting it to make sure that it's not sticking. Continue until you have a thin sheet of dough. Place on a floured baking sheet.

10 Cut the pasta into rectangles, about 6 x 2cm wide. Bring the 1 litre of water to the boil in a large saucepan. Meanwhile, rub the monkfish with the Ají Panca Paste and 1 tablespoon salt.

11 Heat a sauté pan over a high heat, add the olive oil and the monkfish and cook for 6 minutes on each side.

12 When the fish is almost ready, add the pasta to the boiling water and cook for 10 seconds or a little longer if desired. Remove the pasta and place in a bowl. Drizzle with olive oil and season to taste with salt, then mix gently to avoid damaging the pasta.

13 Place the fish and the pasta on a serving plate. Drizzle the Andean Herb Chimichurri and olive oil around the plate and over the pasta. Garnish with herbs of your choice.

Pulpo con Quinua Blanca y Puré de Aceituna Botija

OCTOPUS WITH WHITE QUINOA AND BOTIJA OLIVES

Serves 4

1 octopus, cleaned
(without the head)
240g white quinoa
2 tablespoons olive oil,
plus an extra 2 teaspoons
½ white onion, diced
2 small garlic cloves, chopped
50g Parmesan cheese,
freshly grated
180g Peruvian black
Botija olives
fine sea salt and freshly ground
black pepper
borage flowers, to garnish

1 Fill a large saucepan with water and bring to the boil over a high heat.

2 Meanwhile, place the octopus in a large bowl and rinse under cold running water until the water in the bowl is clear and the octopus skin feels clean, with no traces of grit. Transfer the octopus to a chopping board and cut the tentacles from the body.

3 When the water is at a rolling boil, add the tentacles, stirring gently – they will curl up. Reduce the heat to a gentle simmer, place the lid on top but partially open and cook for 1 hour. Then turn the heat off, cover the pan tightly with the lid and leave to stand for a further hour.

4 Carefully transfer the tentacles to a baking paper-lined baking sheet, cover and refrigerate for a minimum of 3 hours.

5 When ready to serve, rinse the quinoa in cold running water until the water runs clear, then drain.

6 Place the quinoa in a saucepan with a tight-fitting lid and add water to cover by 5cm. Cover with the lid and bring to the boil over a medium heat. Stir, re-cover and reduce the heat to low. Cook for about 15 minutes – the quinoa is ready when you can see a little ring on the outside of the grain and it is soft. Rinse in cold water, then drain well.

7 Heat the 2 tablespoons olive oil in a separate saucepan over a medium-high heat and sauté the onion and garlic until transparent. Add the cooked quinoa gradually, stirring constantly. Season to taste with salt and pepper.

8 Add the Parmesan, stirring until it has melted and mixed in completely. Keep warm.

9 Heat a sauté pan until hot, add the 2 teaspoons olive oil and cook the tentacles until the skin is slightly charred. Keep warm.

10 Place the olives in a blender and blend for 3 minutes, then pass the olive purée through a sieve and set aside until you are ready to garnish the dish.

11 Arranged the cooked quinoa in a line across the dish and top with the seared octopus pieces, then garnish with the olive purée and borage flowers.

Langostinos con Palta y Limón

PRAWNS WITH AVOCADO AND LIME

This dish is a classic Latin American combination and is quick and easy to make. In this healthy and nutritious recipe, two products rich in monounsaturated fat are combined – avocados and olive oil.

Serves 4

1 avocado
1 teaspoon olive oil,
plus 2 tablespoons
1 garlic clove, chopped
16 large raw prawns,
shells on but heads removed
½ teaspoon sea salt flakes
60ml freshly squeezed lime juice

TO GARNISH
parsley and coriander stems
grilled lime slices

1 Cut the avocado in half and remove the stone, then peel the avocado halves and chop into large chunks.

2 Heat a sauté pan over a high heat, add 1 teaspoon olive oil and the avocado and sear for 1 minute on each side. Set the pan aside.

3 Heat a separate sauté pan or a wok over a high heat and let the pan heat up for a minute. Add the remaining 2 tablespoons olive oil and heat until it is shimmering. If it starts to smoke, remove the pan from the heat for a moment.

4 Add the chopped garlic to the pan and toss to coat with the oil off the heat, then put back on the heat and cook for 5 seconds.

5 Add the prawns to the pan and sprinkle with the salt. Toss to coat with the oil. Leave the prawns to cook undisturbed for 2 minutes before tossing again, then add the parsley and coriander and stir-fry for about 2–3 minutes until the prawns are cooked through.

6 Remove from the heat and add the lime juice.

7 Place the seared avocado on a serving dish and pour the pan juices over the warm avocado, then top with the prawns. Garnish with herbs and grilled lime slices, and serve immediately.

Sudado de Coruina

SEA BASS SUDADO

Serves 4

2 tablespoons rapeseed oil

1 red onion, thinly sliced

3 garlic cloves, crushed

2 tablespoons Yellow Ají Paste
(see page 84)

1 tablespoon Ají Rocoto Paste
(see page 87)

3 tomatoes, skinned, deseeded
and chopped

1 tablespoon tomato purée

60ml white wine or chicha de
jora (see page 179)

1 bunch of coriander

4 skinless sea bass fillets

2 tablespoons lime juice

4 chard leaves

fine sea salt and freshly ground
black pepper

BOUQUET GARNI

pinch of dried thyme

2–3 black peppercorns

1 clove

3–4 parsley stems

½ bay leaf

FISH BROTH

25g butter

1 celery stick, chopped

1 carrot, chopped

1 onion, chopped

2kg white fish bones

225ml white wine

4.5 litres cold water

TO GARNISH

sliced shallot

sliced chilli

Sudado is a classic Peruvian dish usually prepared using a fish and shellfish broth incorporating fresh tomato, red onions, yellow chilli and coriander leaves. The fish fillet is cooked in the broth with the other ingredients.

1 Place all the bouquet garni ingredients in the centre of a small piece of muslin, then gather up the corners and tie together with kitchen string to make a bag.

2 To make the broth, heat the butter in a large, heavy-based saucepan over a medium heat. Reduce the heat, then add the celery, carrot and onion, cover and leave to sweat for about 5 minutes or until the onion is softened and slightly translucent. Be careful not to brown the vegetables.

3 Add the fish bones and sweat, covered, for a further 2 minutes until the bones are slightly opaque.

4 Add the white wine and increase the heat until it starts to simmer. Then add the bouquet garni and the cold water and leave to simmer for 30–45 minutes. Strain and leave to cool, then cover and refrigerate.

5 Heat the rapeseed oil in a saucepan over a medium-high heat. Add the red onion and garlic and cook, stirring occasionally, for 10 minutes. Add the Yellow Ají Paste, Ají Rocoto Paste, tomatoes and tomato purée, stirring constantly.

6 Pour in 680ml of the fish broth and the white wine or chicha de jora, then add the coriander and season to taste with salt and pepper. Cover the pan, reduce the heat and simmer the sudado for 15 minutes.

7 Season the fish fillets with salt and pepper, sprinkle over the lime juice and add the fish to the sudado. Leave the fish to cook in the broth for about 7 minutes until it looks slightly opaque. Be careful not to overcook the fish.

8 Cover a serving bowl with the chard leaves, then fill the bowl with the sudado and fish. Garnish with sliced shallot and chilli if desired.

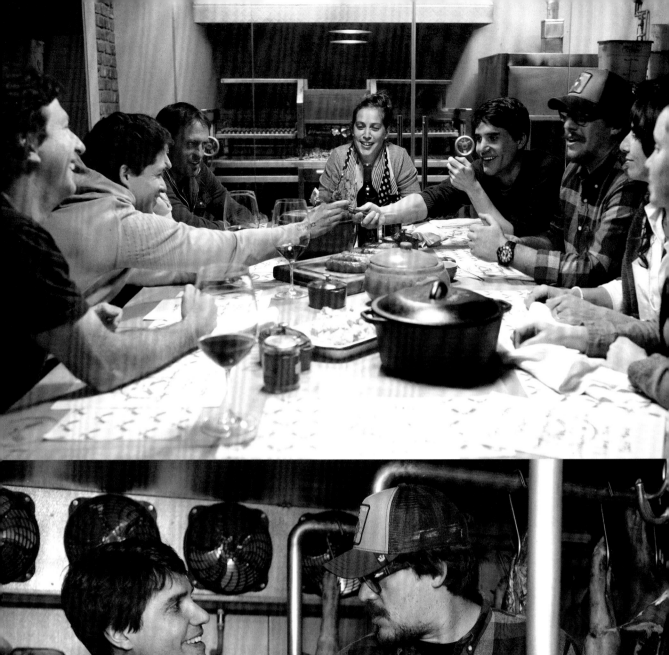

Anticucho de Asado de Tira

SHORT RIB ANTICUCHOS

Anticuchos are Peruvian grilled meat skewers, equally popular as street food available from food carts – *carretilla* – or for cooking on the barbecue at home. The classic anticuchos are made of marinated beef hearts. In Lima there is a celebrated lady called Doña Grimanesa who is famous for her anticuchos – a Peruvian institution!

Serves 4

1.5kg bone-in beef short ribs, ribs separated

1 tablespoon fine sea salt

2 tablespoons Ají Panca Paste (see page 84)

680ml dry red wine

2 heads of garlic, cut in half from top to bottom

2 carrots, chopped

2 yellow onions, cut into quarters

1 small celery stick, chopped into 4 pieces

1 teaspoon peeled and sliced fresh root ginger

½ teaspoon black peppercorns or to taste

½ cinnamon stick

½ small bunch of thyme

300ml cold chicken stock

6 tablespoons red wine vinegar

Huancaína Sauce (see page 89), to serve

1 Cut the ribs into 3cm pieces to assemble on skewers. Generously season on all sides with the salt and the Ají Panca Paste. Leave to marinate at room temperature for 10 minutes. If using wooden rather than metal skewers, leave them to soak in cold water.

2 Meanwhile, boil the red wine in a saucepan until reduced by half. Leave to cool.

3 Light a charcoal barbecue or preheat a gas barbecue.

4 Place the rib pieces in a non-reactive dish and place the garlic, carrots, onions, celery, ginger, peppercorns, cinnamon and thyme on top of the ribs. Add the stock, vinegar and the reduced red wine and leave to marinate at room temperature for a further 10 minutes.

5 Remove the rib pieces from the marinade and thread on to the presoaked wooden skewers or metal skewers. Place them on the barbecue grill and cook, turning frequently, for about 30 minutes until all parts are tender but with a brown crust. Serve with Huancaína Sauce.

Patas de Pavo Glaceado al Ají Panca

AJÍ PANCA GLAZED TURKEY LEGS

Serves 4

4 bone-in, skin-on turkey legs
or drumsticks
55g butter, softened
1 teaspoon fine sea salt
¼ teaspoon freshly ground
black pepper
3 tablespoons Andean Herb
Chimichurri (see page 88)
5 tablespoons Ají Panca Paste
(see page 84)
1 lemon, sliced
2 red peppers, cut in half,
deseeded and cored

TURKEY STOCK

1 turkey carcass
2 celery sticks, roughly chopped
1 large carrot, roughly chopped
1 yellow onion, cut into quarters
1 bay leaf
1 teaspoon black peppercorns

A perfect family dish, this combines the comfort of a classic roast with a touch of Peruvian flavours. The Ají Panca gives a spicy kick and a beautiful red sheen to the turkey legs. Add your own trimmings and favourite roast vegetables for a twist on a Sunday roast.

1 To prepare the turkey stock, break the turkey carcass up with a meat mallet or cleaver so that it fits in a saucepan. Add the celery, carrot, onion, bay leaf and peppercorns, then pour in enough cold water to cover the bones by 5cm. Bring to the boil over a high heat.

2 Reduce the heat and simmer the stock, skimming off any scum that rises to the surface at regular intervals, for about 3 hours or until the broth turns clear. Strain and leave to cool, then cover and refrigerate until required.

3 Preheat the oven to 180°C, Gas Mark 4. Pat the turkey legs dry with kitchen paper and place in a roasting tray.

4 Mix together the butter, salt, pepper, Andean Herb Chimichurri, Ají Panca Paste and lemon slices. Rub this mixture over the turkey legs and under the skin for more flavour. Add the red pepper halves to the tray.

5 Roast the turkey and red peppers for 1½ hours or until a meat thermometer inserted into a leg registers 90°C. The turkey should be light pink.

6 When the turkey is nearly ready, heat 110ml of the turkey stock in a saucepan.

7 Remove the roasting tray from the oven, lift out the peppers and keep warm. Pour the hot stock into the pan with the turkey. Cover and leave to stand for 10 minutes before serving the turkey with the stock and peppers spooned over.

Pachamanca de Gallina y Papas

CHICKEN AND POTATO PACHAMANCA

Serves 4

1 whole chicken, about 2kg,
cut into quarters

3 sweet potatoes, scrubbed and
cut into quarters

3 potatoes, scrubbed and cut
into quarters

kernels from 3 fresh sweetcorn

450ml water

30g huacatay leaves
(see page 88) or coriander,
chopped

3–4 corn husks (see page 106),
optional

PACHAMANCA DRESSING

200g Ají Panca Paste
(see page 84)

3 tablespoons Onion and Garlic
Paste (see page 87)

15g coriander leaves

2 tablespoons dried oregano

40ml white wine vinegar

2 teaspoons fine sea salt

1 teaspoon ground cumin

½ teaspoon freshly ground
black pepper

This is an ancient technique in which cooking takes place underground as a celebration of the *Pacha Mama*, Mother Earth. Traditionally, the meat is marinated in a paste of chilli and other flavourings, vinegar and a wide variety of aromatic Andean herbs. A hole is dug in the ground and stones from the river are heated in a fire until they glow red hot. The hot stones are then placed in the hole, and on top of them the meat and accompaniments. More stones are added to cover, followed by banana leaves or corn husks, then finally the hole is sealed with earth. Here is a recipe adapted for the hob.

1 Place all the dressing ingredients in a blender and blend until smooth.

2 Place the chicken quarters in a non-reactive bowl with the sweet potatoes, potatoes and corn kernels. Add half the dressing and mix to coat well.

3 Cover and leave to marinate in the refrigerator for 2 hours. Cover and chill the remaining dressing in the refrigerator.

4 Layer the ingredients in a large flameproof casserole dish or saucepan in the following order: the 450ml of water, chicken quarters, sweet potatoes, potatoes and corn kernels. Finish by adding the chopped huacatay or coriander and the remaining dressing.

5 Cover with the corn husks, if using, or a circle of baking paper cut to fit the pan, and cover with the lid.

6 Cook for 1 hour over a low heat, keeping the pan sealed to prevent the steam from escaping, until the chicken is cooked through and all the ingredients are tender.

Pastel de Choclo

PASTEL DE CHOCLO

This comforting, sweet-savoury dish was created by nuns and novices of the Catholic Church during Lima's colonial period. It consists of corn *(choclos – see page 52)*, yellow chilli *(Ají)* and a filling of beef stew or rabbit ragout.

Serves 6

6 fresh sweetcorn

40g butter

2 tablespoons Yellow Ají Paste
(see page 84)

1 tablespoon chopped coriander leaves

85ml full fat-milk

3 tablespoons rapeseed oil

4 large onions, finely chopped

3 garlic cloves, finely diced

60g pitted black olives

2 tablespoons Ají Panca Paste
(see page 84)

90g raisins

3kg finely minced lean
salt beef (uncooked)

1 teaspoon ground cumin

1 tablespoon icing sugar

fine sea salt and freshly ground
black pepper

1 Grate the corn cobs on the large holes of a box grater.

2 Heat the butter, grated corn kernels, Yellow Ají Paste, coriander and 1 teaspoon salt in a large saucepan. Add the milk gradually, stirring constantly, until the mixture thickens. Cook over a low heat for 5 minutes. Set aside while preparing the meat filling.

3 Heat the rapeseed oil in a large sauté pan and sauté the onions until transparent. Add the garlic, olives, Ají Panca Paste, raisins and the minced beef and cook, stirring, until browned. Season with salt, pepper and the cumin.

4 Preheat the oven to 200°C, Gas Mark 6. Spread half the corn mixture over the base of a casserole or ovenproof dish to cover it in an even layer. Top with the meat mixture, then spread over the other half of the corn mixture. Sprinkle the icing sugar over the top.

5 Bake, uncovered, for 30–35 minutes until the top is golden brown, then serve.

Virgilio's Tip

This recipe is also very popular with rabbit meat and can be also made with chicken instead of beef.

Sudado de Res

BEEF SUDADO

Serves 4

1 tablespoon olive oil, plus
extra for cooking the beef
1 teaspoon Onion and Garlic
Paste (see page 87)
3 tablespoons Yellow Ají Paste
(see page 84)
3 tomatoes, skinned, deseeded
and chopped
1 tablespoon tomato purée
1 blue potato (see page 14),
peeled and chopped
1 sweet potato, peeled and
chopped
1 bunch of coriander
400g thick slices of beef fillet
fine sea salt freshly ground
black pepper

BOUQUET GARNI

1 tablespoon thyme leaves
2–3 black peppercorns
1 clove
3–4 parsley stems
½ bay leaf

VEGETABLE BROTH

25g butter
1 celery stick, chopped
1 carrot, peeled and chopped
2 white onions, chopped
250ml white wine
2 litres cold water

Sudados are hearty stews that need careful preparation, but with very rewarding end results. In this version, we use chicha de jora, a popular Peruvian fermented drink made with germinated corn kernels. As an alternative, dry white wine or even a light beer instead of chicha de jora would be just as delicious.

1 Place all the bouquet garni ingredients in the centre of a small piece of muslin, then gather up the corners and tie together with kitchen string to make a bag.

2 To make the broth, heat the butter in a large, heavy-based saucepan over a medium heat. Reduce the heat, then add the celery, carrot and onions, cover and leave to sweat for about 5 minutes or until the onions are softened and slightly translucent. Be careful not to brown the vegetables.

3 Add the 250ml white wine and increase the heat until it starts to simmer. Then add the bouquet garni and the 2 litres of water and leave to simmer for 30–45 minutes. Strain and leave to cool, then cover and refrigerate.

4 Heat the olive oil in a saucepan over a medium-high heat. Add the Onion and Garlic Paste and cook, stirring occasionally, for 10 minutes. Add the Yellow Ají Paste, tomatoes and tomato purée, stirring constantly.

5 Pour in 500ml of the vegetable broth, then add the blue potato, sweet potato and coriander. Cover the pan, reduce the heat and simmer the sudado for 15 minutes. Season to taste with salt and pepper

6 Season the beef with 1 teaspoon of salt. Heat a well-oiled sauté pan over a high heat, and when very hot, sear the beef on each side.

7 Add the beef to the sudado broth, cover the pan and cook over a medium heat for 5 minutes before serving.

Pierna Adobada de Cordero Orgánico

SPICY ORGANIC LEG OF LAMB

This is another take on a classic roast, using lamb with a Peruvian touch. The achiote (see page 33) adds a bright colour to this roast, but will not change the flavour of the dish.

Serves 4

400g annatto (achiote) paste or ground annatto (achiote) seeds (see page 33)

1 teaspoon chopped garlic

1 teaspoon grated orange rind

juice of 2 lemons

1 tablespoon chilli powder

1 Ají Limo chilli (see page 83) or jalapeño pepper

2 tablespoons cumin seeds, toasted and ground

2 tablespoons clear honey

1 teaspoon crushed black peppercorns

1 white onion, chopped

1 organic lamb of leg, about 2kg

fine sea salt

1 Mix all the ingredients except the lamb together in a stainless-steel bowl until a paste forms. Add the lamb and thoroughly coat with the paste. Cover and leave to marinate in the refrigerator for 3 hours.

2 Preheat the oven to 190°C, Gas Mark 5.

3 Scrape away any excess paste from the lamb, then place in a roasting tray and roast for about 1¼ hours or until cooked to your liking.

4 Remove the lamb from the oven, cover loosely with foil and leave to rest for 15 minutes before serving.

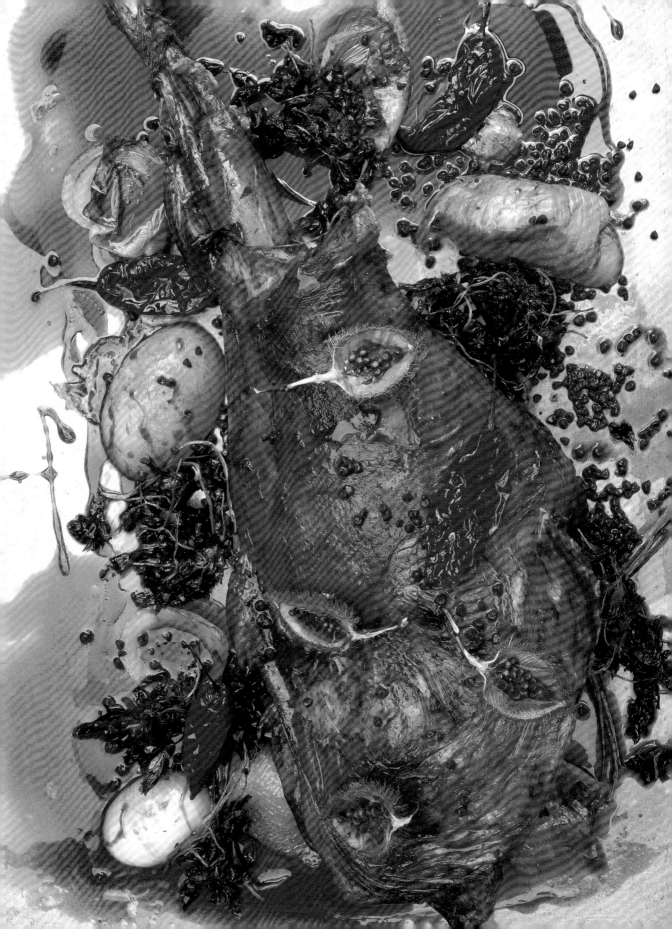

Cerdo con Chicha de Jora

PORK WITH CHICHA DE JORA

Chicha is made from fermented corn. There are both alcoholic and non-alcoholic chichas, and also chichas made from other produce such as quinoa, pineapple and wheat, although corn is most common. The most popular *chichas* are *chicha de jora*, a kind of cider made from yellow corn with a maximum alcohol content of 3 per cent, and *chicha morada*, a sweet soft drink made with purple corn, pineapple and spices.

Serves 4

1 neck end of pork shoulder,
about 3.5kg
900ml chicha de jora or cider
30g caster sugar
3 red onions, chopped
2 celery sticks, chopped
2 carrots, peeled and
cut into chunks
1 tablespoon fine sea salt
2 tablespoons plain flour
500ml vegetable stock
freshly ground black pepper

1 Score the skin of the pork shoulder, then place in a non-reactive dish. Mix 450ml of the chicha de jora or cider with the sugar and pour on to the meat. Cover and leave to marinate in the refrigerator overnight.

2 Preheat the oven to its hottest setting. Place the pork and the marinade in a roasting tray in the oven, then turn the oven temperature down to 190°C, Gas Mark 5, and roast for about 2 hours. Tuck the chopped vegetables under the pork and return to the oven for 15–20 minutes.

3 Baste the pork for the last 10 minutes of cooking. Season well with the salt and black pepper and return to the oven for the remaining cooking time.

4 Remove the pork from the oven, cover loosely with foil and leave to rest for about 20 minutes.

5 To make the gravy, tip the roasting tray at an angle and spoon off most of the fat. Place the tray over a medium heat on the hob and add the flour. Stir it around and cook for a minute or two, then use a potato masher to mash all the vegetables. Add the remaining 450ml chicha de jora or cider and the vegetable stock and cook until reduced to the desired consistency. Pass the gravy through a fine-mesh sieve before serving.

HOME BAKING & DESSERTS

Brioche de Camote

SWEET POTATO BRIOCHE

Playing with a classic French brioche recipe, I made a version using sweet potato that gives the dough a beautiful colour and an added natural sweetness.

Makes 1 large loaf or 20 individual rolls

7g sachet fast-action dried yeast

1 teaspoon caster sugar, plus 2 tablespoons

2 tablespoons lukewarm water

250g sweet potato, baked, peeled and mashed

5 eggs, plus 1 beaten

3 tablespoons full-fat milk

390g plain flour

2 tablespoons fine sea salt

225g cold butter, cut into small pieces, plus extra for greasing

1 Dissolve the yeast and the 1 teaspoon sugar in the measurement lukewarm water.

2 Add the mashed sweet potato to the bowl of a freestanding electric mixer fitted with the paddle attachment and beat for 1 minute on a medium speed. Add the 5 eggs, milk and yeast mixture and beat for 1 minute.

3 Add the flour, the remaining 2 tablespoons of sugar and the salt and mix for about 5 minutes on a medium speed.

4 Leave the dough to rest for 10 minutes, then beat in the cold butter.

5 Remove the bowl from the mixer, cover it with clingfilm and leave the dough to rise at room temperature for about 1 hour or until doubled in size.

6 Gently punch down the dough to release air pockets and reduce its size. Cover the dough and place it in the refrigerator overnight.

7 Remove the dough from the refrigerator and scoop it into a greased 1.4-litre brioche mould, 23 x 12cm loaf tin or 20 muffin cups. Leave the dough to rise at room temperature for about 30 minutes or until doubled in size.

8 Meanwhile, preheat the oven to 220°C, Gas Mark 7.

9 Brush the surface of the dough with the beaten egg and prick it in several places with a skewer.

10 Bake for 10 minutes, then reduce the temperature to 160°C, Gas Mark 3, and continue baking until golden brown, about a further 20 minutes for one large brioche or about 10 minutes for individual rolls. Leave to cool in the mould, tin or cups for 10 minutes, then turn out and leave to cool completely on a wire rack.

Pan de Masa Madre con Quinua Roja

RED QUINOA SOURDOUGH BREAD

This is not a classic sourdough and is a much easier recipe as you will not need to prepare a starter. The red quinoa is the surprise ingredient in addition to the flavour of the rye.

Makes 1 loaf

125g red quinoa, soaked overnight, then drained, cooked and cooled (see page 58)

200g rye flour

200g plain flour, plus extra for dusting

200g wholemeal flour

2 teaspoons fine sea salt

325ml lukewarm water

10g fresh yeast

1 Reserve some cooked quinoa for the topping, then combine the rest of the quinoa with all the other ingredients in a large bowl, cover with a clean tea towel and leave to rest in a warm place for 20 minutes.

2 Turn the dough out on a lightly floured work surface and gently stretch or press the dough into a rough square shape. Grasp the top edge of the dough, then stretch it up and fold about the top third of the dough over on to the remainder of the dough. Now repeat with the bottom edge, then the 2 side edges. Repeat the whole process once more, then return to the bowl to rest for 10 minutes. Repeat this process twice more.

3 Continuing to stretch and fold the dough every 30 minutes for the first 3 hours of the bulk fermenting process (6 times in total).

4 Cover the dough and leave to rest at room temperature for a further 1½ hours.

5 Form the dough into a round and place in a well-floured bowl. Flour the dough well and place the bowl in a plastic bag. Leave to rest in the refrigerator overnight.

6 When ready to bake, preheat the oven to 240°C, Gas Mark 9, and put a deep ovenproof pan with a lid on the middle shelf.

7 Take the dough straight from the refrigerator and turn the loaf out on to a well-floured bread peel or the back of a baking sheet. Sprinkle with the reserved cooked quinoa. Remove the pan from the oven carefully and take off the lid. Slide the loaf into the pan, replace the lid and return to the oven. Bake for 30 minutes, then remove the lid and bake for a further 15 minutes.

8 Remove the bread from the oven and pan, then leave to cool on a wire rack for at least an hour before slicing.

Pan de Cilantro y Cebolla Morada

CORIANDER AND RED ONION BREAD

Speciality breads offer bakers the opportunity to be creative, by turning a simple bread into an exciting dish with the addition of herbs, spices and even vegetables to standard recipes. Here, two classic ceviche ingredients – coriander and red onions – give a twist to a simple white loaf.

Makes 1 loaf

115ml semi-skimmed milk

1½ tablespoons caster sugar, plus extra for sprinkling

15g butter, plus extra for greasing

115ml lukewarm water

2¼ teaspoons fresh yeast

1 tablespoon finely chopped red onion

handful of coriander leaves, finely chopped, plus extra to garnish

170g plain flour

cracked black pepper, for sprinkling

fine sea salt

1 Scald the milk in a small saucepan while constantly stirring. Remove from the heat, add the sugar, 1 teaspoon salt and the butter and mix well until the sugar and salt have dissolved and the butter has melted. Transfer to a bowl.

2 Add the 115ml of lukewarm water to a separate bowl, then add the yeast and mix well. Leave for a few minutes until the liquid begins to froth. Add the onion and coriander and mix well.

3 Combine the flour and both liquids until you have a very sticky dough. Cover the bowl with clingfilm and leave to rise in a warm place for about 45 minutes or until doubled in size.

4 Meanwhile, preheat the oven to 180°C, Gas Mark 4, and grease a 23 x 12cm loaf tin.

5 Knead the dough well and then transfer to the greased loaf tin. Sprinkle with sugar, salt and cracked black pepper and bake in the oven for 1 hour.

6 Turn out on to a wire rack and garnish with extra coriander, then leave to cool.

Focaccia de Chonta y Ajo

HEARTS OF PALM AND GARLIC FOCACCIA

Heart of palms are easily sourced and are often sold in jars or cans. They have a bamboo/artichoke flavour and a soft-cooked white asparagus texture, giving a delicate and slightly sour touch to this bread.

Makes 2–3 breads

700g plain flour

2½ teaspoons fast-action dried yeast

10–12 tablespoons extra virgin olive oil

400–500ml lukewarm water

3 large garlic cloves, peeled but left whole, and 3 unpeeled

150g drained hearts of palm from a jar or can (see page 55), sliced into rings

sea salt flakes

1 Mix the flour with the yeast and add 6 tablespoons of the olive oil and 200–250ml of the lukewarm water.

2 Bring the mixture together with your hands, adding more water, a little at a time, until you have a sticky dough.

3 Knead the dough in the bowl for about 5 minutes, adding a little more olive oil as you go, until it loses some of its stickiness.

4 Add more of the lukewarm water, a little at a time, mixing well with your hands and continuing to stretch and knead the dough until you have a smooth, less sticky dough. Add another tablespoon of the oil while mixing. You may not need all of the water, but the more you can incorporate, the better the aeration of the bread. The mixing and kneading process will take about 15 minutes.

5 Place the dough in an oiled bowl, cover with a clean tea towel and leave to rise in a warm place for about 30 minutes or until doubled in size.

6 Meanwhile, preheat the oven to 150°C, Gas Mark 2. Toss the garlic cloves with a few tablespoons of olive oil and 1 teaspoon sea salt flakes in a roasting tray. Roast for about 45 minutes until the garlic softens and turns golden brown. Set aside.

7 Carefully divide the risen dough into 2–3 pieces, depending on the size of baking tins you are using and the thickness you want. Pat each piece into a shallow baking tin or baking sheet lined with baking paper and well oiled.

8 Push the cooked garlic into the dough and pour over any of the garlic cooking oil in the tin or drizzle the dough with a little extra olive oil. Scatter with the hearts of palm slices and sea salt flakes, cover with clingfilm and leave to rise in a warm place for about an hour until puffy. Meanwhile, preheat the oven 220°C, Gas Mark 7.

9 Bake the bread for 10 minutes, then reduce the temperature to 200°C, Gas mark 6, and bake for 20 minutes. Remove from the oven and drizzle over more olive oil. Serve warm.

Palitos de Pan de Quinua

QUINOA BREAD STICKS

This classic recipe receives a quinoa topping which adds an extra crunch to the sticks. You can also use multicoloured quinoa for a bit of fun!

**Makes about
30 bread sticks**

280g plain flour

60g chickpea
(besan or gram) flour

1 tablespoon fast-action
dried yeast

1 tablespoon caster sugar

1½ teaspoons baking powder

1 tablespoon fine sea salt

340ml lukewarm water

2 tablespoons olive oil

1 tablespoon coconut
palm sugar

1 teaspoon cider vinegar

beaten egg, for glazing

60g white quinoa

1 Place the flours in the bowl of freestanding electric mixer fitted with the paddle attachment, add the yeast, caster sugar, baking powder and salt and mix to combine.

2 Mix together the 340ml of lukewarm water, olive oil, coconut palm sugar and vinegar in a separate bowl.

3 Add to the dry ingredients and beat on a low speed until combined, then increase to medium and beat for 3 minutes.

4 Preheat the oven to 190°C, Gas Mark 5, and line a baking sheet with baking paper.

5 Form the dough into about 30 sticks 20–25cm in length and place on the lined baking sheet about 3cm apart. Cover with a clean tea towel and leave to rise in a warm place for 20 minutes.

6 Brush the sticks with beaten egg to glaze and sprinkle with the quinoa, then bake for 18–25 minutes until golden brown.

Home Baking & Desserts

Queque de Algarrobina

BLACK CAROB POUND CAKE

This simple pound cake becomes an indulgent coffee-time favourite by adding an extra portion of black carob syrup. The syrup, called *algarrobina* in Peru, looks like black treacle and is made from the hard pods of a native tree which can also be ground into a kind of sweet flour or used to make beer. Carob is a highly nutritious vegan product and is also delicious.

Serves 8–10

225g unsalted butter, at room temperature, plus extra for greasing

330g plain flour, plus extra for dusting

340g granulated sugar

4 extra-large eggs, at room temperature

½ teaspoon baking powder

½ teaspoon bicarbonate of soda

1 teaspoon fine sea salt

170ml buttermilk, at room temperature

½ vanilla pod

110ml algarrobina (black carob syrup) or carob molasses, or black treacle for the topping

1 Preheat the oven to 170°C, Gas Mark 3. Grease a 18cm ring tin/mould, then sprinkle with flour and tap to remove the excess flour.

2 Place the butter and sugar in the bowl of a freestanding electric mixer fitted with the paddle attachment and beat for about 5 minutes on a medium speed until light and fluffy. Beat in the eggs, one at a time.

3 Sift together the flour, baking powder, bicarbonate of soda and salt into a large bowl.

4 Add the buttermilk to a separate bowl. Split the vanilla pod in half lengthways, scrape out the seeds from inside the pod into the buttermilk and mix together.

5 Add the dry ingredients and buttermilk alternately to the cake mixture, combining them well.

6 Pour the cake mixture into the prepared ring tin/mould and smooth the top. Bake for 45 minutes–1 hour until a skewer inserted into the cake comes out clean.

7 Leave the cake to cool in the tin/mould for 10 minutes before turning out on to a plate. Top with the black carob syrup or molasses, or black treacle.

Peruvians have a very sweet tooth, as you will soon discover from these recipes! However, if you prefer, you can reduce the sugar content in most instances without detriment to the dessert. Alternatively, to balance the sweetness, add a sour fruit or a dollop of whipped cream.

Banana Caramelizada con Anis Estrella

CARAMELIZED BANANA WITH STAR ANISE

Serves 4

3 tablespoons molasses
or black treacle

5cm piece of cinnamon stick

1 star anise

4 baby bananas, peeled

dried Ají Panca chilli
(see page 83), to decorate

whipped cream, to serve
(optional)

1 Place the molasses or black treacle, cinnamon and star anise in a sauté pan and heat over a low heat.

2 Once the molasses or treacle starts bubbling, add the bananas and cook for 3 minutes until caramelized.

3 Remove the bananas carefully and place each in a serving bowl. Decorate with a piece of dried chilli, if desired, and serve immediately, with whipped cream, if liked.

Suspiro de Manjar Blanco y Ají

CHILLI AND CARAMEL SUSPIRO

Arabian in influence, this dessert was originally called 'white and yellow' because of the colours of the *manjar* or caramel sauce and the meringue. Around the middle of the 19th century, the poet, José Galvez, called it 'sigh of the lady from Lima', since that was where it was created and it's sweet and soft like women from Lima are reputed to be! Today, it's known as *suspiro limeño*. In this version, I have introduced a touch of heat from the red chilli.

Serves 4

CHILLI MERINGUE

60ml water

240g caster sugar

4 egg whites

½ teaspoon chilli powder,
plus extra to decorate

SUSPIRO

2 x 400g cans sweetened
condensed milk

820ml evaporated milk

4 egg yolks

SOFT MERINGUE

300g caster sugar

2 teaspoons port

4 egg whites

2 teaspoons ground cinnamon,
to decorate

1 First make the chilli meringue. Prepare a syrup by heating the 60ml of water with the sugar in a small saucepan, stirring until the sugar has dissolved. Continue heating until it registers 118–121°C (soft ball stage) on a cooking thermometer.

2 While the syrup is heating, whisk the egg whites in a freestanding electric mixer fitted with the whisk attachment until stiff peaks form.

3 When the syrup has reached the required temperature, with the mixer running on a low speed, add the syrup very slowly to the whisked egg whites.

4 Continue mixing on a medium-low speed until the preparation cools to room temperature or until the bowl is lukewarm. Sprinkle the chilli powder into the mixture and mix in.

5 Meanwhile, preheat the oven to 110°C, lowest possible Gas Mark setting.

6 Once the meringue mixture is cool, spread it on to a nonstick baking mat and place in the oven for 4 hours to dry.

7 To make the suspiro, mix the condensed and evaporated milks together in the top of a double boiler over a medium heat until well combined. Reduce the heat and cook, stirring constantly, for 1 hour. The mixture will reduce by 25–35 per cent and turn a light coffee colour.

8 Beat the egg yolks in a bowl, then add a small quantity of the caramel mixture and mix well to prevent the egg yolks from curdling.

9 Gradually add the remainder of the caramel mixture to the yolks, mixing well.

10 Return the mixture to the top of the double boiler and continue cooking for a further 7 minutes, stirring and maintaining a low heat.

11 Pass the mixture through a sieve, then divide between 4 glass serving bowls, filling each with approximately 150ml. Chill in the refrigerator.

12 For the soft meringue, place the caster sugar in a small saucepan and cover with the port. Bring to the boil and heat the syrup until it registers 118–121°C on a sugar thermometer.

13 While the syrup is heating, whisk the egg whites in the mixer until stiff peaks form.

14 Once the syrup has reached the required temperature, remove it from the heat and leave to stand until the bubbles have disappeared.

15 Continue beating the egg whites on a low speed while adding the syrup in visible thin ribbons. Beat on a medium-low speed until the meringue is cool and reduced in volume.

16 Cover each bowl of chilled suspiro with a portion of the soft meringue. Sprinkle with cinnamon mixed with chilli powder and place pieces of the crunchy chilli meringue on top.

Mango Asado con Salsa de Cacao

GRILLED MANGO WITH CACAO SAUCE

Mango and chocolate are a delicious combination. Grilling fruit adds an extra element to desserts, not only visually but also adding a caramelized flavour. On a sunny weekend, why not try barbecuing a selection of fruits for the whole family? As well as mangoes, pineapple, peaches, apricots and figs are perfect for grilling and will taste delicious with the cacao sauce or Chocolate Ice Cream with Chilli Powder (see page 210).

Serves 4

½ vanilla pod
75g cocoa powder
375g caster sugar
300ml water
canola oil, for oiling
4 ripe mangoes

TO SERVE (optional)
cacao nibs (see page 23)
thin tuile biscuits
finely sliced dried Ají panca
chilli, to decorate

1 Split the vanilla pod half in half lengthways and scrape out the seeds from inside the pod.

2 Place the cocoa, sugar and the 300ml of water in a saucepan over a medium heat, bring to the boil and continue boiling for 1 minute. Remove from the heat and stir in the vanilla seeds. Set aside.

3 Preheat a griddle pan or a gas barbecue to a medium-high heat, or light a charcoal barbecue. Oil the griddle pan or barbecue grill.

4 Meanwhile, slice through each mango either side of the central narrow stone to cut away the 2 halves of the fruit, discarding the stone. Peel the mango halves.

5 Place the mango halves directly on the hot griddle pan or barbecue grill so that you get grill marks on the fruit. Leave to cook for 7 minutes.

6 Serve the grilled mangoes with a small dish of chocolate sauce, with cacao nibs, thin tuile biscuits and dried Ají panca chilli, if desired.

Crema de Café con Chirimoya

COFFEE CREAM WITH CHERIMOYA

Serves 4

500g ripe cherimoya
(custard apple – see page 25)
60g butter, diced
4 tablespoons crushed
rich tea biscuits
4 tablespoons rolled oats
mint leaves and borage flowers,
to decorate

COFFEE CUSTARD

1 tablespoon plain flour
2 tablespoons cornflour
1 tablespoon cocoa powder
225ml full-fat milk
225ml freshly made
espresso coffee
40g caster sugar

COFFEE CREAM

3 egg yolks
65g caster sugar
20g cornflour
50ml full-fat milk
50ml single cream
100ml freshly made
espresso coffee
50ml coffee granules
150ml double cream, whipped

Virgilio's Tip

You can freeze cherimoya whole and eat it as an ice cream without doing anything else to it. Maybe it's for this reason that some people have given it the nickname 'ice cream fruit'.

1 Peel the cherimoya and discard the seeds, then cut the flesh into 1cm pieces. Chill in the refrigerator.

2 Preheat the oven to 160°C, Gas Mark 3.

3 To make the coffee custard, mix the flour, cornflour and cocoa powder with half the milk in a bowl to make a paste. Set aside.

4 Place the remainder of the milk in a saucepan with the espresso coffee and 4 tablespoons of the sugar. Heat over a low heat, stirring, until the sugar has dissolved.

5 Stir a little of the hot milk into the chocolate paste and mix well, then add the chocolate paste to the milk mixture in the pan.

6 Bring to the boil and cook, stirring constantly, until thickened. Pour the custard into a baking dish.

7 Rub together the butter, biscuit crumbs, oats and remaining sugar in a bowl and scatter over the coffee custard. Bake for 20 minutes, then leave to cool.

8 Meanwhile, make the coffee cream. In a bowl, mix the egg yolks with the sugar and cornflour. Put the milk, single cream, espresso and coffee granules into a small saucepan and stir over a low heat until the mixture reaches 90°C on a sugar thermometer. Add a little of the mixture to the egg yolk mixture and stir, then pour all the egg yolk mixture into the saucepan and heat, stirring constantly, for 20 minutes or until it becomes thick and creamy. Remove from the heat, then fold in the whipped cream.

9 In a vase or large glass bowl, make layers in the following order: first the crumble, then the coffee cream, then the chilled cubes of cherimoya and finish with more crumble. Add mint leaves and borage flowers to decorate before serving.

Quinua y Leche de Cabra con Fresas

QUINOA AND GOAT'S MILK PUDDING WITH STRAWBERRIES

This is a Peruvian version of rice pudding and can be served as a breakfast/brunch dish or as a dessert. You can add your favourite fruits and double cream.

Serves 4

110g white quinoa

125ml water

100g caster sugar

pinch of fine sea salt

1 tablespoon cornflour

1 large egg

375ml goat's milk

25g butter

1 teaspoon vanilla extract

110g strawberries, cut into quarters

110g blueberries

handful of mint leaves and borage flowers

1 Rinse the quinoa in cold running water until the water runs clear, then drain.

2 Place the quinoa and measurement water in a saucepan with a tight-fitting lid. Cover and bring to the boil over a medium heat. Stir, re-cover and reduce the heat to low. Cook for about 15 minutes – the quinoa is ready when you can see a little ring on the outside of the grain and it is soft.

3 In a large saucepan, whisk together the sugar, salt and cornflour. Add the egg and whisk well. Whisk in the milk and add the cooked quinoa.

4 Heat the milk mixture over a medium-high heat, stirring constantly, until boiling. Allow to bubble for 30 seconds and then remove from the heat.

5 Stir in the butter and vanilla extract. Leave the pudding to cool, uncovered, for about 30 minutes.

6 Serve the pudding decorated with the strawberries, blueberries, mint leaves and borage flowers.

Parfait de Nuez de Bahuaja

BAHUAJA NUT PARFAIT

In Peru, Bahuaja nuts (same as Brazil nuts) are collected from January to April in Bahuaja Sonene, the National Park near the border with Bolivia. It is an ecologically protected area and many Peruvian chefs and artists are friends of the park, trying to raise awareness of the need to protect this important area of unique biodiversity. This dessert is my celebration of the Bahuaja nut.

Serves 4

100g dextrose powder
20g liquid glucose
20g caster sugar
90g milk powder
1 litre full-fat milk
250g shelled Bahuaja nuts
(Brazil nuts), roughly chopped,
plus 100g grated, to decorate
2½ leaves of gelatine

1 Place the dextrose, glucose, sugar, milk powder and milk in a saucepan and heat until it registers 85°C on a sugar thermometer.

2 Transfer the milk mixture to a blender, add the chopped nuts and blend until well combined, then pass through a sieve into a saucepan.

3 Soak the gelatine leaves in a bowl of cold water for 5 minutes or so.

4 Drain and squeeze out the excess water from the leaves, then add to the nut milk mixture. Gently heat until it registers 50°C on a sugar thermometer and the gelatine has completely dissolved.

5 Pour the mixture into a freezer-proof serving dish, cover and place in the freezer for about 2 hours until firm.

6 Serve decorated with the grated nuts.

Sorbete de Mango

MANGO SORBET

There are many varieties of mango available. Sometimes they are sold unripe and green, but there are a number of tricks that will help ripen them. First, avoid mangoes with bruises, black pigment around the stem or black spots. Mangoes are tropical fruits and they need a warm temperature to reach their full flavour and aroma, so never place a green mango in the refrigerator. Keep mangoes in your fruit bowl at room temperature or in a warm place. For this sorbet, you will need ripe, soft fruit.

Serves 4

2 large mangoes
300ml water
200g caster sugar
juice of 1 lemon
1 egg white

Virgilio's Tip

If you don't have an ice cream machine, prepare the mixture and freeze in a covered freezer-proof container for 40 minutes–1 hour. Stir vigorously, then return to the freezer. Repeat the process at least 5 times to avoid ice crystals forming for a smoother mixture.

1 Slice through each mango either side of the central narrow stone to cut away the 2 halves of the fruit, discarding the stone. Cut a criss-cross pattern into the flesh of the mango halves to create cubes. Bend the skin of each half backwards to separate the cubes, then cut the cubes from the skin.

2 Place the mango cubes in a food processor and process until smooth. Pass through a sieve and refrigerate until ready to use.

3 Pour the 300ml of water into a saucepan, add the sugar and heat gently, stirring occasionally. When the sugar has dissolved completely, increase the heat a little and bring to the boil, stirring constantly. Boil for 1 minute, then set aside to cool completely.

4 Stir the sugar syrup into the mango purée, and then stir in the lemon juice.

5 Whisk the egg white in a bowl until soft peaks form, then gently fold into the mango mixture.

6 Pour the mixture into an ice cream machine and churn according to the manufacturer's instructions. Transfer to a freezer-proof container, cover and freeze until ready to serve. Transfer the sorbet to the refrigerator for 15–30 minutes before serving.

Helado de Chocolate y Ají

CHOCOLATE ICE CREAM WITH CHILLI POWDER

Serves 8

270g caster sugar

40g cocoa powder

600ml semi-skimmed milk

3 large egg yolks, lightly beaten

70ml double cream

70g plain dark chocolate, chopped

1 teaspoon Ají Panca chilli powder (see page 83) or cayenne pepper

Virgilio's Tip

If you don't have an ice cream machine, prepare the mixture and freeze in a covered freezer-proof container for 40 minutes–1 hour. Stir vigorously, then return to the freezer. Repeat the process at least 5 times to avoid ice crystals forming for a smoother mixture.

1 Combine the sugar and cocoa in a heavy-based saucepan over a medium-low heat. Add 100ml of the milk and the egg yolks and stir well.

2 Stir in the remaining milk and cook for 12 minutes or until it registers 160°C on a sugar thermometer, stirring constantly. Remove from the heat.

3 Place the cream in a microwave-proof bowl and heat in a microwave oven on high for 1½ minutes or until the cream boils. Add the chocolate to the cream and stir until smooth.

4 Add the chocolate cream mixture to the pan and stir until smooth. Place the bowl in a large, ice-filled bowl and leave to cool completely, stirring occasionally.

5 Pour the mixture into an ice cream machine and churn according to the manufacturer's instructions. Transfer to a freezer-proof container, cover and freeze for 1 hour until firm or until ready to serve.

6 Sprinkle the chilli powder on top just before serving.

Helado de Quinua con Chips de Papa

QUINOA ICE CREAM WITH POTATO CRISPS

Serves 8

340ml Quinoa Milk (see page 29)

225ml double cream

100g caster sugar

2 tablespoons golden syrup

1 vanilla pod

3 large egg yolks

1 potato (I use blue potatoes)

225ml rapeseed oil

fine sea salt and freshly ground
black pepper

1 Follow the method on page 29 to prepare the Quinoa Milk.

2 Place the cream, half the sugar, the golden syrup, a pinch of salt and the quinoa milk in a heavy-based saucepan.

3 Split the vanilla pod in half lengthways and scrape out the seeds from inside the pod. Add the seeds and the pod to the cream mixture. Heat the cream mixture until it registers 180°C on a sugar thermometer or until tiny bubbles form around the edge (do not boil). Remove the pan from the heat, cover and leave to stand 10 minutes.

4 Place the remaining 50g sugar and the egg yolks in a bowl and stir well with a whisk. Gradually add the hot cream mixture to the egg mixture, stirring constantly with the whisk.

5 Transfer the mixture to a saucepan and cook over a medium heat, stirring constantly, until it registers 160°C on the sugar thermometer. Remove from the heat.

6 Place the pan in a large, ice-filled bowl for 20 minutes or until the mixture is cool, stirring occasionally. Pour the mixture through a fine-mesh sieve into an ice cream machine, discarding the solids, and churn according to the manufacturer's instructions. Transfer to a freezer-proof container, cover and freeze for 3 hours until firm or until ready to serve.

7 Preheat the oven to 200°C, Gas Mark 6. Peel and thinly slice the potato into a bowl, then immediately toss with the oil. Season the potato slices lightly with salt, then arrange in a single layer on a baking sheet. Reduce the oven temperature to 180°C, Gas Mark 4, and bake for about 12–15 minutes until golden brown.

8 Season again lightly with salt and with pepper, then transfer to a wire rack to cool and become crispy.

9 Serve the quinoa ice cream in cups, each topped with potato crisps.

Chocolate Crudo y Muña

RAW CHOCOLATE WITH MUÑA MINT

Cacao Butter is made from milled cacao beans. The roasted beans are ground to a paste which is pressed until a thick and creamy butter is extracted. Muña, also known as Andean mint, is a shrub with great aromatic and medicinal value. It grows in Peru at high altitudes from 2,700 to 3,100 metres. In this recipe, you can use regular fresh mint if you can't source fresh muña.

Makes 300g

115g raw cacao butter

2 tablespoons coconut oil

3 tablespoons soft light brown sugar

2 tablespoons raw honey

1 tablespoon cocoa powder

1 small bunch of muña mint or any mint, leaves only, washed, dried and chopped

1 Prepare a bain-marie (hot water bath) by standing a heatproof bowl in a large saucepan of hot water. Add the cacao butter, coconut oil, sugar and honey to the bowl and wait for the ingredients to melt, being careful not to overheat them, as this will destroy some of the nutrients. Ideally, you want to keep the mixture below 43°C.

2 Once all the ingredients have melted, whisk in the cocoa powder.

3 Set the bowl over a pan of cold water, being careful to avoid getting any water inside the bowl. Continue to whisk constantly until the mixture starts to thicken. The raw honey and the oil tend to separate, so you need to keep mixing until the mixture has cooled a little.

4 Pour the raw chocolate mixture into a shallow baking tin lined with baking paper.

5 Sprinkle the chopped mint over the chocolate mixture.

6 Place in the freezer for a couple of minutes and then transfer to the refrigerator for 1 hour or until set.

Achiote
See Annatto or achiote seeds

Aguaymanto
See Physalis or Aguaymanto.

Ají
This term applies to all the various types of Capsicum (a genus of the Solanaceae family), both sweet peppers and hot chilli peppers. Chillies and other peppers are the very foundation of the Peruvian culinary tradition, and pages 82–83 give a guide to those most widely used in the country.

Aloe vera
The spiky leaves of this succulent plant (*Aloe barbadensis miller*) contain an edible flesh with a gelatinous, sticky texture. Aloe gel boasts 19 amino acids, including seven of the eight essential ones, and besides its nutritional value, it has long been used for medicinal purposes. Its ability to heal burns was recognized 4,000 years ago.

Amaranth or kiwicha
As its nickname 'mini quinoa' indicates, this is a pseudo-cereal like quinoa but with a smaller size of grain, and is noted for its rich nutritional content. *Kiwicha* has been farmed in Peru and other areas of South America for over 4,000 years.

Annatto or achiote seeds
These powerful red/orange-coloured seeds are found inside pods of the achiote tree (*Bixa orellana*). The seeds produce the carotenoid bixin, a naturally occurring pigment, when they are mature. The native communities of the Amazon use the seeds to make body paint, colour hair and dye textiles. It is also used in many Peruvian cooking preparations, such as spice pastes.

Anticucho
These are Peruvian barbecued meat skewers – see page 166.

Bahuaja or Brazil nut
In Peru, Bahuaja nut kernels, known around the world as Brazil nuts, encased within tough fruit pods are harvested from Brazil nut trees (*Bertholletia excelsa*) in the Bahuaja-Sonene National Park in the Madre de Dios region, near the border with Brazil, from January to March. The nuts are packed with protein, fibre and essential fats.

Black or American carob
The hard pods of this native tree (*Prosopis pallida*) that grows in the wild in the arid forests of northern Peru are harvested from January to April and used to make a type of syrup or molasses called algarrobina. Highly nutritious, the pods can be also ground into a sweet flour or used to make beer.

Blue potato
There are 20 varieties of blue or purple-coloured potatoes (*Solanum andigenum*), among them the Purple Peruvian, a finger-shaped variety. The colour comes from the high level of flavonoids that the potatoes contain, with their beneficial antioxidant properties.

Cacao or cocoa nibs
These are cocoa beans – the seeds of the cacao or cocoa tree (*Theobroma cacao*) – that have been roasted and broken into little pieces. They contain high levels of magnesium and iron, and have a bitter taste and crunchy texture.

Cancha corn
These are large-sized kernels from a special variety of corn or maize (*Zea mays*) that pop when roasted but don't puff up like regular popcorn; they are deliciously crunchy instead. The most popular snack in Peru, cancha corn is often served alongside ceviche. See also Chullpi corn.

Cañihua
This species of goosefoot (*Chenopodium pallidicaule*), like its better-known relative quinoa, is cultivated as a grain crop and used in the same way. It has a high protein content and is rich in health-promoting antioxidants.

Cassava, manioc or yuca
The starchy root of the cassava plant (*Manihot esculenta*) is widely used in Latin American and African countries. In Peru, it is mainly served cooked and is also used to make the Peruvian alcoholic beverage masato or chicha de yuca.

Causa
This is a traditional type of Peruvian dish, based on a highly seasoned dough of mashed yellow potatoes and formed into a pie, cakes or smaller savouries (see page 129).

Ceviche or cebiche
The most emblematic Peruvian dish, ceviche consists of marinated cubed raw fish fillets served with its citrusy, spicy marinade known as tiger's milk (see page 75).

Chancaca

This is a natural, unrefined sugar resulting from the filtered raw juice of the sugar cane being gradually cooked down to a dark crystallized form. In Peru, many desserts are prepared with chancaca syrup, made from chancaca, water, orange rind and spices.

Cherimoya or chirimoya

The small tree or shrub (*Annona cherimola*) that yields the cherimoya fruit is believed to be native to the Andes, although it grows in many Latin American and Mediterranean countries and Spain is now the largest producer of cherimoya in the world. With a sweet yet slightly tart flavour, its 'meaty', creamy flesh has given rise to its alternative name of custard apple (see page 24).

Chia seeds

Harvested from a flowering plant of the mint family (*Salvia hispanica*), chia seeds are a valuable source of dietary fibre together with antioxidants, calcium, protein and omega-3 fatty acids.

Chicha

This term refers to Peruvian drinks produced from the fermentation of products rich in starch and/or sugar, such as corn or maize (see Chicha de jora) and other grains, potatoes and other tubers (see page 179). There are non-alcoholic chichas as well as alcoholic ones, such as chicha morada. In ancient times, chicha was served at religious ceremonies.

Chicha de jora

This is an alcoholic beverage made from fermented sprouted corn grains, or jora, that have been sun-dried and then ground. The ground grains are boiled with water, then left to ferment for few days with or without the addition of the unrefined sugar chancaca (see above).

Chicha morada

A popular non-alcoholic drink made by boiling together purple corn, pineapple skin, quince, apple, cinnamon and cloves.

Chifle

This dish consists of fried slices or strips of ripe or green plantains seasoned with salt. The flavour can be either sweet, if using ripe plantain, or savoury, using green plantain.

Chilcano

A classic Peruvian cocktail made from pisco, Angostura bitters, freshly squeezed lemon juice and ginger ale.

Chimichurri

A sauce widely used in South America, particularly Argentina, Paraguay and Uruguay, the ingredients include parsley, oregano, garlic, vinegar, salt and vegetable oil. It is mainly served as an accompaniment to grilled meats but is also used in sandwiches or to marinate fish or chicken.

Chirimoya

See Cherimoya or chirimoya.

Choclo

This Peruvian white sweetcorn or maize (*Zea mays*) from the Andes has large, pale-coloured kernels.

Chonta

See Hearts of Palm or chonta

Chullpi corn

These are small-sized kernels of corn or maize (*Zea mays*) similar to cancha corn, which keep their shape and become crunchy when deep-fried. As with cancha corn, chullpi corn is a snack beloved by Peruvians and often served with ceviche.

Escabeche

This dish usually features deep-fried fish fillets or marinated chicken, and is traditionally accompanied by hard-boiled eggs, queso fresco, boiled sweet potato and black olives. It can be served warm or cold.

Hearts of palm or chonta

Also called palmito and pupunha, hearts of palm are the edible inner cores from the stems of various species of palm tree (see page 55).

Huacatay

The most important Peruvian herb, huacatay (*Tagetes minuta*) can be found growing wild on the coast as well in the Andes and jungle, but is widely cultivated in domestic gardens in Peru. Its unique aroma can be compared to a mixture of coriander, mint, tarragon and parsley (see page 88). It is an integral part of many national dishes and sauces such as pachamanca (see page 171) and ocopa (see page 90).

Huancaína

This name is given to any dish prepared using huancaína sauce, a yellow creamy sauce made from queso fresco, cream, Ají Amarillo chilli, red onions and seasoning (see page 89).

Jalea mixta

A mixture of deep-fried assorted seafood, jalea mixta invariably features among the traditional seafood dishes on Peruvian menus.

Jora

This is the term for corn kernels that have been allowed to sprout (germinate) for the purposes of making chicha de jora.

Kión

This is the Spanish word for the rhizome of the ginger plant (*Zingiber officinale*) – fresh root ginger.

Kiwicha
See Amaranth or *kiwicha*.

Lúcuma
The lucuma tree (*Pouteria lucuma*) grows in the valleys of the Andes at an altitude of 2,500 metres and produces large, oval-shaped fruits with a diameter of some 10cm. Their mostly yellow/orange-coloured flesh is highly aromatic and nutritious, with an earthy texture.

Muña
This aromatic herb (*Minthostachys mollis*) native to Peru grows at an altitude of between 2,000 and 4,000 metres and has mint-like notes.

Ocopa
An ocopa, a pouch filled with peanuts seasoned with chillies and herbs, was reputedly carried by messengers of the Incan empire to fortify them on their missions, and today, ocopa sauce (see page 90) uses these same ingredients. It is particularly associated with the city of Arequipa in southern Peru.

Pachamanca
The technique used in the preparation of this dish has been practised in Peru since pre-Hispanic times whereby marinated meat is cooked in the ground using hot stones, like an underground oven, for several hours (see page 171).

Paico
This aromatic herb (*Dysphania ambrosioides*) is one of the flavourings traditionally used in the preparation of pachamanca, and grows in temperate, sub-tropical and tropical climates. It is also used medicinally to treat a variety of ailments.

Palmito
See Hearts of palm or chonta.

Physalis or aguaymanto
The physalis plant (*Physalis peruviana*) is indigenous to South America, but has been cultivated in Britain since the late 18th century, and in South Africa in the Cape of Good Hope area for nearly as long, hence its alternative name Cape Gooseberry. Its yellow berry-like fruits found inside a papery calyx contain numerous small seeds and have a distinctive sweet-sour flavour.

Pisco
The national Peruvian drink with a designated Denomination of Origin, pisco is a distillation made from grapes – see page 36.

Pisco sour
This is the national cocktail of Peru prepared with pisco, fresh lemon juice, simple (sugar) syrup, egg white and Angostura bitters (see page 37).

Pupunha
See Hearts of palm or chonta

Purple corn or maiz morado
This dark purple-coloured corn or maize (*Zea mays*) originates from the Andes. It is the main ingredient of the soft drink chicha morada.

Purple corn chicha
See Chicha morada

Queso fresco
This is a type of soft, creamy-white curd cheese made mostly from cow's milk but can also be made from a combination of cow's and goat's milk.

Quinoa
The quinoa plant (*Chenopodium quinoa*) is a species of goosefoot that produces small, nutritious seeds in a variety of colours, the most popular of which are black, red and white. Regarded as a superfood, quinoa is an excellent source of protein and essential amino acids.

Salsa criolla
A type of red onion relish dressed with vinaigrette, this is served as an accompaniment to many Peruvian dishes (see page 93).

Sudado
This renowned Peruvian dish is prepared using a fish and shellfish broth – see page 162.

Suspiro
One of the best-loved traditional Peruvian desserts, suspiro combines rich caramel sauce with creamy meringue (see page 198).

Tiger´s milk or leche de tigre
This is the name given to the citrus-based marinade that is used to cure the fish in a ceviche (see page 75).

Tiradito
This Peruvian dish of raw fish is comparable to Japanese sashimi or Italian crudo or carpaccio, with the addition of a spicy sauce (see page 114).

Uchucuta
The ingredients of this classic Peruvian sauce include chillies, peanuts, Andean herbs and queso fresco. It is traditionally made using a batán, a stone mortar.

Yuca
See Cassava, manioc or yuca.

Our Restaurants

LIMA Fitzrovia
31 Rathbone Place
London W1T 1JH
Tel. 020 3002 2640
www.limafitzrovia.com

LIMA Floral
14 Garrick Street
London WC2E 9BJ
Tel. 020 7240 5778
www.limafloral.com

www.twitter.com/lima_london
www.instagram.com/lima_london
www.facebook.com/limalondonfloral
www.facebook.com/limarestaurant

Central Restaurante
Calle Santa Isabel 376 Miraflores,
Lima, Peru
Tel.+511 242 8515
www.centralrestaurante.com.pe

Stockists

Andess
www.andess.eu
*Peruvian food specialist, selling
dried ají panca chillies, corn.*

Buy Whole Foods Online
www.buywholefoodsonline.co.uk
*Online store selling nuts; seeds;
hearts of palm; exotic fruits;
vegetables and herbs.*

Brixton Market
London SW9
*Daily market selling exotic fresh
fruits; roots and tubers; blue /purple
potatoes; cassava (yucca); aloe vera.*

Carroll's Heritage Potatoes
www.heritage-potatoes.co.uk
Supplier of blue potatoes.

Fine Food Specialist
www.finefoodspecialist.co.uk
*Online specialist for hard-to-find
quality produce, including oca
tubers and blue/purple potatoes.*

Healthy Supplies
www.healthysupplies.co.uk
*Online health food store selling
cacao nibs; raw cacao butter;
amaranth and quinoas.*

Holland & Barrett
www.hollandandbarrett.com
Stores nationwide.
*Health food specialist selling
quinoa; chia seeds; nuts and other
superfoods.*

La Bodeguita
www.labodeguita.co.uk
*Restaurant and deli in South London
and online Latin American food
store selling a good selection of
Peruvian products including corn,
grains and flours.*

Melbury & Appleton
www.melburyandappleton.co.uk
*Independent online food store
selling all kinds of International
foods including ají chillies and
annatto (achiote) paste.*

Morghew Gourmet Potatoes
www.morghewgourmetpotatoes.com
Supplier of blue/purple potatoes.

Quinola
www.quinola.com
*Online store specializing in quinoa
and quinoa-based products.*

Real Foods
www.realfoods.co.uk
*Online store selling nuts; seeds;
vegetables and herbs.*

Rico Picante
www.ricopicante.co.uk
*Online store with a good selection of
ready-made chilli sauces.*

Sol Andino Market
solandinomarket.co.uk
*Online Peruvian food specialist,
selling dried chillies; corn; grains,
including quinoa; ready-made ají
pastes and spices.*

Sous Chef
www.souschef.co.uk
*Online store with a wide variety of
International produce, including
annatto (achiote) paste.*

Viva Peru
www.vivaperu.co.uk
*Online store with a good selection
of ready-made pastes; dried
chillies; cancha corn; corn husks;
algarrobina (black carob syrup).*

Whole Foods Market
www.wholefoodsmarket.com
Stores nationwide.
*Nuts; seeds; palm hearts; exotic
fruits; vegetables and herbs.*

A very big thank you to the LIMA team for all their hard work and dedication to Peruvian food. I am very grateful to all members of my family, who support me and from whom I have learned a great deal. They remind me of the importance of remaining in contact with one another, even at a distance, and of not losing a connection with our roots. In our work, guided by these thoughts, we have been able to develop projects like the LIMA restaurants and *The LIMA Cookbook*. We have unlimited possibilities to promote our culture through gastronomy, as we see it, always keeping in mind the values of a Peruvian family, just like mine.

Virgilio

LIMA has been an incredible adventure which has changed the lives of the people involved. We are honoured that the hard work and effort we have put into it has had such a positive welcome by the public. We are thrilled to continue writing this great culinary story. A massive thanks to the dedicated team of people that make it happen every single day. We want to give a special mention to Leila and Jose Luis Gonzalez who with devotion, confidence, trust and financial support made the founding partners' dream come true. Along with them the Herrera-Mendoza family who with passion, knowledge and consistent financial backing have been a key pillar of the LIMA project. We cannot be more thankful to them.

Gabriel and Jose Luis

A BIG thank you to: the Central team: Karime, Peter and Maribel for your hard work. To James, Palmiro, Roberto, Diego, Renzo, Malena, Pia, Renato, Micha, Toshiro, Esther at ID LIMA Barcelona, and the beautiful people of Surquillo and San Isidro market who kindly helped us during the photo shoot in Lima. To Erick for your commitment and dedication. To Alison, Jonathan, Sybella and the Octopus team for making timeless, authentic and relevant books. To Pene for your beautiful work – you are the best! To my dear Gregory Smith for your friendship – you always make me feel at home in Peru. To Iain, my tireless editor and friend – I keep learning from you everyday! I dedicate this book to my dear Julie and Clive – you are always with me, wherever I am in the world.

Luciana

Virgilio Martinez was the national champion of Peru in skateboarding in the 1990s, but after an accident he decided to study law in Lima. During a holiday job, he discovered a passion for cooking, dropped out of university, and travelled first to Canada and then to London to become a chef. Returning home, he opened his own restaurant, Central, in the Peruvian capital in 2010, now the number one restaurant in Peru (according to Summum, Peru's leading restaurant guide), and recently voted the number one best restaurant by Latin America's 50 Best Restaurants list and 4th in The World's 50 Best Restaurant ranking.

The 36-year-old chef also has two restaurants in London – LIMA Fitzrovia and LIMA Floral – celebrating informal modern Peruvian cooking. LIMA is the UK's first and only Peruvian restaurant to be given a Michelin star.

www.limalondon.co.uk
www.instagram.com/limalondon
www.twitter.com/limalondon

Luciana Bianchi is a food writer and trained chef with a background in molecular science. She has worked in Michelin-starred restaurants, cooked for celebrities, interviewed most of the top international chefs, and has published work in 14 countries.

Luciana is a member of the Guild of Food Writers UK, a contributor to the website of The World's 50 Best Restaurants, and a writer for the Italian International Food Guide, *Identità Golose*.

A frequent traveller and food researcher based in the UK, she divides her time between Latin America and Europe. With more than 20 years experience in the field, she is a gastronomy consultant for M&C Saatchi, and an Associate Lecturer at the Basque Culinary Centre. Luciana is co-author of the award-winning book *Brazilian Food* (Mitchell Beazley).

www.luciana-bianchi.com
www.instagram.com/lucianabianchi
www.twitter.com/lucianabianchi